THE ORGANIZATIONAL FORM OF FAMILY BUSINESS

THE ORGANIZATIONAL FORM OF FAMILY BUSINESS

by

Stefan P. Bornheim

University of St. Gallen, Switzerland

Kluwer Academic Publishers
Boston/Dordrecht/London

Distributors for North, Central and South America:
Kluwer Academic Publishers
101 Philip Drive
Assinippi Park
Norwell, Massachusetts 02061 USA
Telephone (781) 871-6600
Fax (781) 871-6528
E-Mail <kluwer@wkap.com>

Distributors for all other countries:
Kluwer Academic Publishers Group
Distribution Centre
Post Office Box 322
3300 AH Dordrecht, THE NETHERLANDS
Telephone 31 78 6392 392
Fax 31 78 6546 474
E-Mail <orderdept@wkap.nl>

Electronic Services <http://www.wkap.nl>

Library of Congress Cataloging-in-Publication Data
Bornheim, Stefan P.
    The organizational form of family business / by Stefan P. Bornheim.
        p.cm.
    Includes bibliographical references and index.
    ISBN 0-7923-7939-X
    1. Family-owned business enterprises--Econometric models. 2. Family-owned
business enterprises--European Union countries--Econometric models. I. Title.

    HD62.25.B67 2000
    338.7--dc21

                                                        00-058419

TABLE OF CONTENTS:

List of Figures ix

List of Tables x

1. INTRODUCTION 1

1.1 FAMILY BUSINESS 2

1.2 GROUNDED THEORY 3

1.3 ORGANIZATIONAL ECOLOGY 5

1.4 THE GENERAL SCOPE OF THIS RESEARCH 6

1.5 OUTLOOK 9

2. LITERATURE REVIEW 11

2.1 FAMILY BUSINESS 11

   2.1.1 Definitional issues *13*

   2.1.2 Statistics *14*

   2.1.3 Succession *17*

   2.1.4 International family business research *19*

   2.1.5 Entrepreneurship links *22*

   2.1.6 Strategy *24*

   2.1.7 Organizational behavior *26*

   2.1.8 Questions unanswered... .... *27*

2.2 GROUNDED THEORY 29

   2.2.1 Basic considerations *29*

   2.2.2 Some thoughts on the qualitative/quantitative dichotomy *32*

   2.2.3 Grounded theory in contrast to other methodological approaches *34*

      2.2.3.1 The inherent characteristics of qualitative research 35

      2.2.3.2 The benefits of grounded theory 36

      2.2.3.3 Triangulation 37

      2.2.3.4 The use of cases and case studies 38

   2.2.4 The hard core vs. the periphery *41*

   2.2.5 Some more philosophy of science... .... *45*

      2.2.5.1 Sir Karl R. Popper 45

      2.2.5.2 Thomas S. Kuhn 46

      2.2.5.3 Paul K. Feyerabend 47

2.3 ORGANIZATIONAL ECOLOGY 48

   2.3.1 Central themes *50*

2.3.1.1 Adaptation and selection 51

2.3.1.2 Density dependence 53

2.3.1.3 Organizational foundings 55

2.3.1.4 Organizational mortality 55

2.3.1.5 Further categories of ecological research 55

2.3.2 Questions remaining 56

2.3.3 The fit of grounded theory and organizational ecology 58

2.4 THE EUROPEAN UNION 59

2.4.1 The institution and process of the European Union 60

2.4.2 Chronology of the Union 61

2.4.3 The history of the Union 63

2.4.4 The evolution of the European Union 64

2.4.5 The democratic foundations of the European Union 64

2.4.6 The single market in 1995 65

2.4.7 Small and medium-sized enterprises in the European Union 65

2.5 A SUMMARY OF IMPLICATIONS FOR THIS RESEARCH 66

3. METHODOLOGY **67**

3.1 FORMAL DESCRIPTION 68

3.1.1 The procedure 68

3.1.2 The cases 74

3.2 BASIC GROUNDED THEORY PROCEDURES 76

3.2.1 Theoretical sensitivity 76

3.2.2 The use of literature 76

3.2.3 Coding procedures in grounded theory 77

3.2.3.1 Open coding 77

3.2.3.2 Axial coding 77

3.2.3.3 Selective coding 77

3.3 THE SECONDARY DATA 78

3.3.1 The INTERSTRATOS project 79

3.3.2 The questionnaire 80

3.3.3 The data 81

3.3.4 Statistical techniques 81

3.3.5 Testing for assumption violations 82

3.3.5.1 Heteroskedasticity 82

3.3.5.2 Multi-Collinearity 83

3.3.6 Statistical procedures 84

3.4 THE UTILIZATION OF GROUNDED THEORY AND ECOLOGICAL CONJECTURES IN
FAMILY BUSINESS 85

4. RESULTS..89

4.1 PRESENTATION OF CASES 89
   4.1.1 Austria (case A)...90
   4.1.2 Denmark (case D) 90
   4.1.3 Germany..91
      4.1.3.1 Case G1 91
      4.1.3.2 Case G2 91
      4.1.3.3 Case G3 91
   4.1.4 Sweden (case S1) 92
   4.1.5 Switzerland (case S2)...92
4.2 THE MODEL...93
4.3 THE CORE ELEMENTS AS FOUND EMBEDDED IN THE CASE DATA 95
4.4 THE STATISTICAL ANALYSIS OF THE INTERSTRATOS DATA...........................99
   4.4.1 The hypotheses 100
   4.4.2 Variables and proxy constructs 101
      4.4.2.1 Hypotheses concerning the individual core elements 102
      4.4.2.2 Hypotheses concerning the whole core model...........................104
   4.4.3 Descriptive data set information...104
   4.4.4 Results and presentation of the statistical analysis.........................105
      4.4.4.1 1991 (IS91)...108
      4.4.4.2 1992 (IS92)...115
      4.4.4.3 1993 (IS93)...121
      4.4.4.4 1994 (IS94)...127
      4.4.4.5 1995 (IS95)...135
      4.4.4.6 Summary of significant results 142

5. DISCUSSION...145

5.1 THE REFINED MODEL...145
   5.1.1 Simplicity..148
   5.1.2 Focus on core business...151
   5.1.3 Dedication, enthusiasm and belief...152
   5.1.4 Values and principles 153
   5.1.5 Incentives and rewards...154
5.2 VALIDATION OF THE REFINED MODEL THROUGH INTERSTRATOS...............155

5.3 CAVEATS...159

5.4 FUTURE RESEARCH 162

5.5 SUMMARY AND CONCLUDING QUESTIONS 163

6. BIBLIOGRAPHY **169**

Index **183**

List of Figures:

FIGURE 1: FAMILY FIRMS IN SWITZERLAND 15
FIGURE 2: FAMILY FIRMS IN WEST GERMANY...16
FIGURE 3: CASE MATRIX 39
FIGURE 4: THE ADAPTATION VS. SELECTION DILEMMA 52
FIGURE 5: THE EVOLUTION OF THE EUROPEAN UNION 63
FIGURE 6: FAMILY BUSINESS CORE, PERIPHERY AND ENVIRONMENT 94
FIGURE 7: FAMILY BUSINESS CORE ELEMENTS...95
FIGURE 8: THE REFINED FAMILY BUSINESS CORE MODEL.....................................146
FIGURE 9: THE "FAMILY BUSINESS TIE"..162

List of Tables:

TABLE 1: CHRONOLOGY OF THE EUROPEAN UNION..62
TABLE 2: CASE STATISTICS..75
TABLE 3: DATA SET DESCRIPTIVE STATISTICS...81
TABLE 4: CASE DEMOGRAPHICS..93
TABLE 6: DATA SET VARIABLES LABEL, NAME AND SCALE...............................102
TABLE 5: DATA SET SUMMARY STATISTICS..105
TABLE 7: LOGIT REGRESSION RESULTS FOR INTERSTRATOS 1991....................110
TABLE 8: PROBIT REGRESSION RESULTS FOR INTERSTRATOS 1991..................113
TABLE 9: LOGIT REGRESSION RESULTS FOR INTERSTRATOS 1992...................117
TABLE 10: PROBIT REGRESSION RESULTS FOR INTERSTRATOS 1992...............119
TABLE 11: LOGIT REGRESSION RESULTS FOR INTERSTRATOS 1993................123
TABLE 12: PROBIT REGRESSION RESULTS FOR INTERSTRATOS 1993..............126
TABLE 13: LOGIT REGRESSION RESULTS FOR INTERSTRATOS 1994................130
TABLE 14: PROBIT REGRESSION RESULTS FOR INTERSTRATOS 1994..............133
TABLE 15: LOGIT REGRESSION RESULTS FOR INTERSTRATOS 1995................137
TABLE 16: PROBIT REGRESSION RESULTS FOR INTERSTRATOS 1995..............140
TABLE 17: COMPARATIVE SIGNIFICANCE STATISTICS 1991-1995........................143

THE ORGANIZATIONAL FORM OF FAMILY BUSINESS

> ... this is the problem with the value of discourse in comparison with intuition ... in that language is a convenient, pragmatic method that - yet debilitates the realization and *adaequatio* of the cognition, which hence dilutes the complete awareness... (Teilhard de Chardin SJ, 1916)[1]

1. INTRODUCTION

The purpose of this chapter is a) to introduce the concepts of family business (section 1.1), grounded theory (section 1.2), and organizational ecology (section 1.3); b) to explain how grounded theory will be used to develop an evolutionary theory of family business based on organizational ecology (section 1.4); and c) to provide a bridge to chapter two's in-depth review of the developments and uses of those concepts (section 1.5). In these five sections (1.1-1.5), those insights from Henry Mintzberg's talk at the 1996 Academy of Management Annual Meetings (Cincinnati, August 9-13, 1996), which are particularly applicable to their respective topics will be presented.

More important to Mintzberg than the insights he expounded was the passion he found wanting in his peers and consequently strove to instill in his audience. He contended that most of his fellow academics lacked passion for their work because of their daily preoccupations with lectures, committees, reviews, and so on. It is hoped, therefore, that this manuscript will not only advance understanding of Mintzberg's contribution to the discussion and field, but will also inspire more passionate involvement in the academic process and the pursuit of greater understanding.

---

[1] de Chardin 1995:160, translation by the author

1

1.1 Family business

Family business (FB) is the central unit of analysis in this research project with particular focus on family business as an organizational form. Family business as a research field has received increased attention recently, especially through the integrative efforts of scholars in the entrepreneurship field[2].

As family business is a rather young field, there is currently no theory or framework in the discipline. The first formal organization established in the field was the Family Firm Institute in the U.S. (1986) followed by the first academic journal (Family Business Review) in 1987. Similar efforts led to the creation of the Family Business Network (1990) in Europe (at the IMD, Lausanne). Thus considering its heritage and youth, one can find a wide area of people interested in this field: a) family therapists/ psychologists/ counselors, b) family business owners (and members), c) family business consultants, and d) academicians/researchers.

These circumscribing and historical statements are necessary to understand why previous research in family business has been mostly descriptive, anecdotal, or consultative and oriented toward the applied and practical side of the family business, not the development of a comprehensive theoretical framework.

The majority of the more theoretical research that is or has been carried out on family business deals with the sole issue of succession, which at first glance may seem overly focused or unbalanced.

However, consider for example the implication of the following statistics for the German economy. According to conservative estimates of the IFM research institute in Bonn, of the current 2.3 million entrepreneurs in the former West Germany, 13% or 299,000 would have had to have dealt with succession by the year 2000[3]. This conservative figure excludes any family business considered likely to either be bought out by another company or integrated into a newly founded firm; for the remaining families, however,

---

[2] Brockhaus, 1994a; Brockhaus, 1994c; Donckels & Fröhlich, 1991; Dyer & Handler, 1994; Hoy & Verser, 1994

[3] Freund, Kayser & Schröer, 1995:59

succession is not an option, but a decision that needs to have been resolved by now[4].

Clearly, the economic implications of these statistics more than justify the immense interest of researchers in family business succession.

However, there are more issues in and about family business that are yet to be explored and certainly because of their magnitude of economic power further inquiry seems justified and warranted.

As Mintzberg demanded of every research journal article written, implicitly pointing to the current lack thereof: Research and its results must be thoughtful and applicable to practitioners!
Hence, what better dictum for carrying out this research to better understand how family businesses operate.

1.2 Grounded theory

Grounded theory (GT) entered the academic arena of methodological approaches with the publication of Glaser & Strauss's book "The Discovery of Grounded Theory" in 1967[5]. Grounded theory was proposed as a methodological innovation in the field of sociology.
Positioned against theories generated by logical deduction from *a priori* assumptions, this theory is a stringent qualitative methodology of inquiry without any pre-conceived notions[6].
Simply stated, grounded theory aims to generate theory by formulating research processes embedded in the data. Or, to use a catchy expression which clearly reflects the position taken by this innovative theory within the philosophy of science, grounded theory aims to *theorize from data*, whereas other methodologies aim to *generalize from data*.

As the reader may deduce from the above phrase, grounded theory suggests that every subsequent grounded theory study would come up with a new theory. Glaser & Strauss argue that a) every new "little" theory adds

---

[4] Freund et al., 1995
[5] Glaser & Strauss, 1967
[6] Glaser & Strauss, 1967:3

sufficient new knowledge, in that it is considered valid until refuted, and b) the marginal contributions of these new theories may well lead to, and at some point add up to a more generalizable, grand theory[7].

So as this research attempts to develop an evolutionary family business theory, positioning family businesses as a distinct organizational form (based on conjectures from organizational ecology), an open and uninhibited playing field – achieved through utilizing a grounded theory methodology – heightens chances for observing precisely how family businesses behave. The instance of how a family business makes sense of an ever-changing environment will be used to develop a more general theory of the family business form. With the use of the verb "sensemaking", intentional reference is made to Karl Weick's work on sensemaking in organizations, to clearly distinguish it from action-implying or theory-laden verbs such as adapting or coping (see especially his introductory section on defining the concepts)[8].

In addition to the above mentioned reasoning on the utility of grounded theory, which was inferred from the research literature, the methodology also allows the field researcher to in Mintzberg's words, "be surprised by the ordinary". This might help explain the success of family business, which previous research has not elaborated on in any systematic or theoretical fashion.

Arguably, organizational theory is moving towards a search for explanatory power in more complex systems, or what has also been termed complexity theory[9]. But other researchers are moving in the opposite direction, the direction of simplicity pointed out by Mintzberg[10]. Two outstanding examples, particularly in the German context are the publications of Simon[11] and Rommel et al.[12], with Rommel's book oddly enough entitled 'Simplicity

---

[7] Glaser & Strauss, 1967; Strauss & Corbin, 1990
[8] Weick, 1995:4-6
[9] cf. McKelvey, 1996
[10] Mintzberg, 1996
[11] Simon, 1996
[12] Rommel et al., 1995

Wins' (published 1996 in the Harvard Business School Press); these studies will be elaborated on in later parts of this book.

1.3 Organizational Ecology

The theory intended for use in this research was originated in the late 1970's by Hannan and Freeman[13] in their seminal article 'The Population Ecology of Organizations' and also by Aldrich[14], and now called 'Organizational Ecology'[15]. The theory of organization ecology – with a focal point on selection – can be considered an adversary to the more adaptation focused theories. For example Porter's five forces theory allows the firm to pro-actively position itself and adapt in a rapidly changing environment[16]. In ecology, emphasis is placed on understanding the diversity of organizational forms (such as family business) and its implications[17]. Organizational ecology is being developed and utilized by researchers from a rather wide array of disciplines, particularly organization theory, entrepreneurship, and sociology.

The theory of organizational ecology was chosen for this study because it encompasses the following perspectives:
a) a population perspective in the research, i.e. an aggregated organizational dimension, rather than a more individualistic perspective as is offered by the popular theory of Porter[18] or others,
b) given that organizational ecology is not only a theory of evolution but furthermore an evolving theory itself, it provided enough flexibility within the research framework and also potential room for theory development, which was essential considering the family business field could not provide for any self-standing theories[19],

---

[13] Hannan & Freeman, 1977

[14] Aldrich, 1979

[15] Hannan & Freeman, 1989

[16] Porter, 1985; Porter, 1990

[17] Lomi, 1995a

[18] Porter, 1990

[19] the aforementioned evolutionary flexibility of organizational ecology was part of the reason why other theories such as Porter's Model cf. Porter,

c) recent research in organizational ecology began addressing issues that could be of central importance to this research:

    A.   issues of concern in other organizational research such as organizational learning and innovation are being examined upon their fit, compatibility and necessity within the organizational ecology paradigm[20],

    B.   the necessary distinction between the hard core and periphery of an organization and its implication for the success or failure of an organization are being elaborated on[21].

Concluding again with a thought by Mintzberg, who challenged his audience in Cincinnati not to be the best, but to be good, because being the best might be too low a standard, thus your own standards should prevail. Regarding organizational ecology then, regardless of the quantitative or qualitative advances a research paradigm develops, it should never become inert and too complacent with its achievements. By taking on new ventures such as the question of the fit of organizational learning with organizational ecology, Mintzberg's challenge is being answered.

1.4 The general scope of this research

This section sets forth in very general terms how grounded theory will be used to develop an evolutionary theory of family business based on organizational ecology as a distinguishable organizational form.

This section attempts a comprehensive conclusion of what has been detailed in the previous subsections, i.e. bringing together these unrefined parts into a whole picture, before proceeding into a detailed literature review in the next chapter.

1985; Porter, 1990, contingency theory cf. Lawrence & Lorsch, 1967, transaction cost economics cf. Williamson, 1975; Williamson, 1993, or institutionalism cf. Meyer & Rowan, 1977; North, 1990 were dismissed

[20] on learning cf. Bruderer & Singh, 1996; Levinthal, 1991; Levinthal, 1995; Levinthal & March, 1993

[21] Ginsberg & Baum, 1994; Hannan & Freeman, 1989

First, a few words must be spent on the only aspect of the phrase 'evolutionary family business ecology' not yet detailed. The word 'evolutionary' in organizational research is mostly associated with evolutionary theory which is broader in scope and distinct from organizational ecology but nevertheless related and overlapping.

The use here of the evolutionary notion signifies simply that the model to be developed will be evolutionary in nature, allowing for the principles of variation and selection/retention to be assumed, while also providing for the principles of self-organization and autopoieses.

Arguably, the aforementioned argument is not as refined as an evolutionary theorist might prefer it to be; however, the assumptions of organizational ecology regarding its underlying principles are not inclusive enough for the purpose of this study, and thus are enhanced by the addition of some evolutionary rationale.

The application of grounded theory methodology permits the research team to select various family firms in Europe (i.e. the European Union). The rationale behind this decision will be outlined in detail in section 2.4 on page 59.

Because of the implications of grounded theory methodology, it is important to recall the methodology procedures before an initial number of firms is selected, contacted and permission requested and the actual research carried out.

Once the companies agree to the initial request, the researchers then visit the company to talk and discuss a semi-structured catalog of questions with the designated people.

This very procedure of talking with family business members permits the new theory development. In a positivistic mind-set one theory of explanation exists, and the only point of visiting a company would be to empirically validate the theory. However, through the action of grounded theory, new processes – possibly quite divergent from existing theory – are to emerge from the collected data, the interviews.

Realistically, not all conjectures of the new theory development will have emerged for the first time; i.e., certain principles and assumptions, albeit not consciously retained, may re-surface after an initial analysis of the collected data.

Particular conjectures must be attributed to their origin, which nevertheless will not diminish their importance in the new theory or the significance of the new theory.

This scientific inquiry set forth to build a new family business theory based on conjectures from organizational ecology, of which many have applicability in certain organizational settings. Yet, the authority of adding explanatory power to a new family business theory by employing existing organizational ecology conjectures is by no means diminished.

For example, the notion of hard core and periphery of an organizational form, is certain to emerge from the data collection, but it is already in use in the organizational ecology framework and thus cannot be claimed new. Nevertheless, this conjecture of core and periphery may prove very integral in the development of the new theory.

However, the prescriptions provided by organizational ecology on what core and periphery mean in an operationalized manner[22], may not be validated or may even be refuted by the new theory.

Actually, the very concept of hard core and periphery is not even inherently original to organizational ecology. As a matter of fact, the idea stems from contemporary philosophy of science literature, particularly as developed by Imre Lakatos[23].

Despite the fact that the notion of family business so far has only been written about in abstract terms – with the definitional discussion forthcoming in section 2.1.1 on page 13 – the central importance of organizational form to the study of family business can still be emphasized. The intention here is to suggest that through the participatory observation of family business in their process of retrospective sensemaking, new insights could be gained not only on cognition issues, but also of structures as well

---

[22] Hannan & Freeman, 1989:79-80

[23] Lakatos & Musgrave, 1970

as processes (in both instances informal and formal). Extended knowledge on behaviors, motives, thought processes and motivation may also be anticipated.

This section was intended to provide an overview on how the three distinct aspects of grounded theory, organizational ecology and family business tie together in the development of a new theory. The very step of stringing together these three elements leads to the conclusion of this section with a last thought of Mintzberg.

Mintzberg asserted that this world is too complex for a single lens. And with this clear criticism of any positivistic research programs he went on to propose that multiple perspectives are necessary to understand the complexity of today's reality.

Thus, regarding this research project, one may safely assume Mintzberg's approval of the mixing of the various school of thoughts, and research methodologies and units of analysis.

1.5 Outlook

After this introductory chapter a literature review will ensue, beginning with a review of family business research. This is followed by a discussion of family business definitional issues, and accompanied by some data to exemplary show the economic importance of family business in Germany and Switzerland.

Next, a review of the research literature on grounded theory, its developments, and its epistemological and ontological assumptions in the view of contemporary philosophy of science will follow.

A literature review and historical outline of organizational ecology including the theoretical achievements will be provided. Also, a comparison to the other main organizational theories, justifying the theory selection, will be offered.

As was briefly indicated earlier, the geo-political choice of the research setting was Europe and the European Union, respectively. The objective and rationale of this decision will be pointed out.

Concluding from this literature review is the derivation of the research question, which will occur through the indication of the potential shortcomings in the extant literature, in addition to outlining where the pursuit of the stated research question will help advance our current knowledge and the progression of the overall research program.

2. LITERATURE REVIEW

In chapter one, a general overview of the scope of the research was given, which will be followed up now, with an extensive literature review.

This literature review will give an overview of the developments in the various research areas and outline deficiencies in the existing strand of research literature, showing how some of these deficits can be remedied and how the proposed research work is justified within these scientific research programs.

2.1 Family business

The field of family business is a rather young academic field of inquiry, uniting a diverse group of people, such as family therapists, psychologists, counselors, family business owners, family business members, family business consultants, attorneys, accountants, tax specialists, academicians and researchers. The first U.S. (United States) research conference solely dedicated to family business issues was held in the fall of 1985. The first formal organization established in the field was the Family Firm Institute in the U.S. (1986) followed by the first academic journal (Family Business Review) in 1987. Similar efforts led to the creation of the Family Business Network (1990) in Europe (at the IMD, Lausanne, Switzerland).[24]

With these globe-spanning organizations in place, regular – mostly annual – conferences came about. Although there is some overlap in participation, the three organizations generally target distinct interests. The U.S.-based Family Firm Institute serves mostly family business support institutions, such as lawyers, accountants, consultants and family therapists, while the Switzerland-based Family Business Network mostly seeks its audience among family business owners and family business members. A third conference is organized by the U.S.-based International Family Business Program Association and is mainly directed towards academicians and researchers. In any case, none of these groups is exclusive and so the described foci are just emphasis. At each gathering, one will find representatives almost of all the groups mentioned above.

---

[24] Lansberg, 1995

In light of these historical statements, it can now be understood why research in the area of family business has been mostly descriptive, anecdotal, and consulting oriented, that is, focused towards the applied and practical side of the family business, and not at all towards the development of a comprehensive theoretical framework[25].

However, signs of recent research concentration in the family business area can be seen in the increased number of dissertations[26], special journal issues[27] and special bibliographic collections[28].

In the diversity of backgrounds and lack of theoretical framework, the evolution of the family business field parallels that of the entrepreneurship field[29].

Prior to the evolution of the family business field in the mid-1980's, occasional articles on family business issues were published in the literature.[30] However, it is notable that much of this earlier literature was hostile to the combination of family and business, suggesting that the organizational form of family business was inherently detrimental to the success of the venture, and advocated dissolving of the family connection and involvement in the firm[31]. With these earlier attributions to the negativity of the family and business connection, it must be acknowledged now that the recent research on family business for the most part assumes that the organizational form of family business is inherently positive and desired; a distinct assumption the reader must be made aware of.

After this 'historic' general introduction, the next part is comprised of detailed reviews of the research literature along functional and topical lines.

---

[25] cf. Goffe, 1996

[26] cf. Lansberg, 1995

[27] such as the *Entrepreneurship: Theory & Practice* special issue on family business in 1994

[28] a debt of gratitude is owed to Harold Welsch for availing his newest Family Business Bibliography prior to official publication; Welsch, 1997

[29] Lansberg, 1995

[30] Gersick, 1994a

[31] Donnelley, 1988; Hollander & Elman, 1988:146; cf. Gersick, 1994b

2.1.1 Definitional issues

A sure sign that a research paradigm's development is still nascent is if it lacks agreement on the basic definitions[32]. The field of entrepreneurship went through its fair share of debate on entrepreneurs and entrepreneurship; although little agreement was reached, a sort of academic pragmatism with each researcher specifically stating his/her own definition at the beginning of each new manuscript was achieved[33]. Unfortunately, this makes any kind of constructive and comparative efforts practically impossible.[34]

The developments in the family business arena are similarly frustrating. Indeed, Lank recently remarked that as many definitions of family business exist as there are family business researchers[35].

To avoid discussion of this large number of definitions, the reader may be directed to a recent study by Litz, in which he examines these past definitions, and tries to synthesize the definition along three chosen dimensions. First, he proposes a uniting statement along the criteria of ownership and employment. A second proposition involves the criterion of intentionality, while the third proposition synthesizes the first two.[36]

While this integrative effort deserves praise, the added complexity and vagueness poses new problems, particularly in terms of operationalization.

For the purpose of this study, however, a definition of what constitutes a family business needed to be provided. The criteria of choice were:

1. reputation and experience of the provider,
2. applicability of definition in cross-cultural study setting, and
3. encompassing, yet simple enough for operationalization.

---

[32] Lakatos, 1970

[33] Katz, Brockhaus & Hills, 1993

[34] for further enlightenment on the history and divergence of entrepreneurship definitions the reader may attend to Mugler, 1995

[35] Lank, 1996

[36] Litz, 1995

13

Through the review of a number of definitions a final choice was made for Alden Lank's definition. His academic definition is:

a family business is a company in which a given family controls the voting equity.[37]

This definition satisfies all three conditions. Lank's reputation and commitment to the field of family business is undisputed; he is the initiator of the Family Business Network, held (until 1999) the Schmidheiny Professorship of Family Enterprises, and directed an educational program for family business members at IMD. The definition moreover allows usage across different national boundaries, yet is simple enough to allow operationalization in the field.

The above definition is used only for this study, while the studies reviewed in the further context used different and diverging definitions of family business.

2.1.2 Statistics

A number of the authors cited in this literature review, reiterated the importance of the family business for the economy. Contributive characteristics mentioned were:

- percentage number of family firms vs. total firms
- percentage of gross domestic product contributed by family firms
- percentage of total employment and jobs created by family firms
- providers of economic stability.

As an exemplary overview of the importance of family businesses globally the following statistics are provided. According to the most recent reports 90% of Chilean firms are family controlled, while Mexico has a 80% family business rate. In the United States 95% of all corporations are family controlled. In Italy 99% of all firms are considered family firms.[38]

---

[37] Lank, 1996
[38] Ward & Mendoza, 1994:3

In the Netherlands the family business rate is about 52%, while the Austrian and Spanish rates exceed 80%.[39]

For two of the five countries involved in the case research, the following more detailed statistics regarding the number of family firms were available. The figures for Switzerland are depicted in Figure 1.[40]

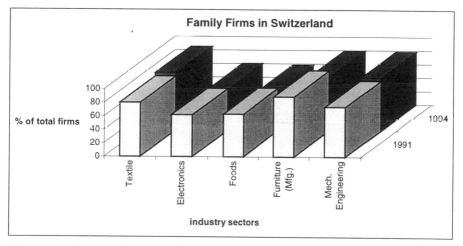

Figure 1: Family Firms in Switzerland

Based on a representative sample from five industries, the above figure indicates that about 75% of the firms in Switzerland are family firms. Although exact figures for employment level or job creation could not be obtained, within the timeframe of the above two observations (1991, 1994) no significant change in the number of family firms can be observed. Hence, a confirmation of family business stability may cautiously be assumed.

---

[39] Anonymous, 1994; Kets de Vries, 1996:3

[40] cf. Brunner, Habersaat & Pleitner, 1995:15

Since these numbers merely serve as a point of illustration, no further detail discussion on the data source, sampling procedures and representativeness of industries will be provided.

Complete population statistics are available from Germany, as seen in Figure 2[41]. The completeness however, means that the most recent figures date back to 1990 and subsequently are only available for West-Germany. Also no comparative trend figures were available.

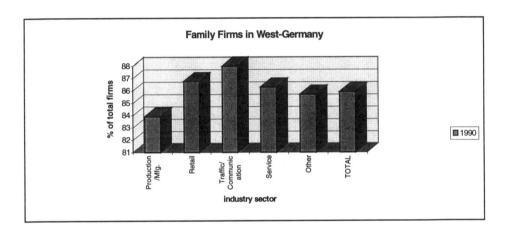

Figure 2: Family Firms in West Germany

Comparing the percentage of Germany's and Switzerland's family firms, a similarly large relative number is evident. Both values are in line with general expectations. Higher values have been quoted for Italy, Spain and the U.S. (above 85%)[42], but caution must be used in comparing these relatively static numbers without delineating the methodological differences in the various surveys. Additional numbers, such as employment share and

---

[41] cf. Freund et al., 1995:21

[42] Anonymous, 1994

gross domestic product share would help elevate these statistics to a more meaningful comparison.

2.1.3 Succession

When the issue of family business arises, most people automatically associate the issue of succession. The reasons for this phenomenon are manifold. For one, because of the family nexus, succession is the only problem solely inherent to the organizational form of family business. Second, most people do not think or perceive of certain firms as family businesses, until the issue of succession arises; this too often is even the case with family business owners. And thirdly, the vast majority of popular press publications and research articles on family business concern themselves with the issue of succession[43].

With succession also comes the issue of generational status and transition, which is of natural concern to the study of family business. For the mere purpose of illumination the following statistical figures are provided. Through prior research it has been established that roughly speaking only about 30% of the businesses pass from the first to the second generation, and only 10% of these firms make it into the third generation[44]. More exact survival rates are available but vary across countries. For a European perspective on these issues see Donckels and Fröhlich[45].

And while succession remains to be the major matter in family business, this particular research study does not concern itself with family business succession. The interested reader may be directed to the most recent known and complete study by Handler. She reviewed 108 studies concerning family business succession prior to 1994, organized them into five categories, distinguished several major themes (succession as a dynamic process; the role of the founder or retiree; and the successor's viewpoint),

---

[43] for a most recent exemplar cf. Zaudtke & Ammerman, 1997
[44] Kets de Vries, 1996:5
[45] Donckels & Froehlich, 1991

and pointed to research questions in need of further scientific investigation.[46]

In regards to the non-U.S.-focused literature, a number of exemplary European studies will now be delineated.

A study by Bechtle advocated the preservation of the family business form because of the economic impact of family businesses. She further assessed the need to employ successors based on their qualifications and not their relationship to the family.[47]

Spielman found that succession in medium-sized companies is particularly troublesome if the transfer occurs from the first to the second generation, a problem he attributes to the special personality characteristics of the founding entrepreneur and which may be remedied according to specific guidelines.[48]

Bergamin examined the options in the succession process and found that relinquishment of the firm via sale is often the only option. His study proceeds to detail an operational plan for this process.[49]

Rik Donckels, in another study, compared his survey from Belgian family business executives to the themes of Handler, and suggests that in the dynamic process of succession the importance of emotions and their suppression is often misjudged. His advice to the retiring founder is pragmatic in that he suggests they arrange to be financially secure for life. He also suggests that successors analyze their own desires to succeed and become entrepreneurs, and the implications of this step and new role. Lastly, he proposes the installment of a family charter to serve as an overarching, guiding set of principles.[50]

Another country specific example is provided by Crijns et al. They examine the transition process of medium-sized firms in Belgium[51], while Kuratko et al. compares family firm succession in Korea to the U.S.[52]

---

[46] Handler, 1994; cf. Handler & Kram, 1988

[47] Bechtle, 1983

[48] Spielmann, 1994

[49] Bergamin, 1994; Bergamin, 1995

[50] Donckels, 1996a; Donckels, 1996b

[51] Crijns, Ooghe & Cosaert, 1994

A last acknowledgment should go to the existence of the many popular press articles dealing with family business succession. These articles are mostly based on individual case studies and lack the analytical depth of research. For a good common sense example confer Wohlgemuth.[53]

2.1.4 International family business research

The purpose of this section is to discuss notable family business research conducted outside the U.S.

The first professorial chair in family business in Europe is held by Miguel Gallo (at IESE, University of Navarra, Spain). He remains a prolific writer on family business topics such as the contribution and importance of the family business to the economy, particularly in Spain[54]. He followed this research by further examining the Spanish industrial infrastructure and pointing out the prominence of family businesses among the largest firms in Spain[55]. Gallo then ventured into the more behavioral aspects of the family business and explored the role of wives in the business, as well as non-family managers[56]. Another issue of inquiry became that of internationalization; and while Donckels and Fröhlich[57] had previously shown that family firms are slow to internationalize (implying conservativeness and stability-orientation), Gallo further analyzed the factors underlying this slow process of realizing the need to internationalize.[58] Gallo's recent research studied financing aspects of the family business[59].

Another person whose essential efforts helped to establish the present family business framework is Alden Lank. He helped found the Family Business

---

[52] Kuratko, Hornsby & Montagno, 1993

[53] Wohlgemuth, 1993

[54] Gallo & Pont, 1988

[55] Gallo & Estape, 1992a; Gallo & Estape, 1995

[56] Gallo, 1990; Gallo, 1991

[57] Donckels & Froehlich, 1991

[58] Gallo & Estape, 1992b; Gallo & Pont, 1993

[59] Gallo & Vilaseca, 1995

Network and his research on the definitional issue of family business is noteworthy.[60]

Two similarly prominent European family business researchers are Rik Donckels and Erwin Fröhlich. They co-authored several studies, regarding whether family businesses are substantially different from other types of firms. Based on the data from the longitudinal eight country study STRATOS, they found that family businesses tend to be more inward directed and strategically conservative, making family firms an economic stabilizing factor, rather than a progressive force.[61]
Donckels also examined the environment and hurdles facing family firms on their way to the next millennium, and found that there is no 'right' way to clear these hurdles, but hard work and the need for awareness[62].
Fröhlich further refined the differentiating characteristics of family firms, and found that the family firm in trade and crafts is an important economic factor, but that through the diminishing role and value of the family in society, its economic contribution and stabilizing effect is also endangered.[63]
Watkins examined the relevance of the human resources management literature to the family business from a British perspective, and concluded that the mainstream human resources management practices are not applicable to family owned businesses. Rather, he postulated, the application of strategic human resources management to the family business should be easier because of six reasons, including the strong family business culture, less unionization, and greater flexibility.[64]

While reviewing international family business research, an acknowledgment should be made to the publication of "Global Perspectives on Family Business", which evolved from a conference of the same name held at Loyola University. The publication contains papers that deal with a variety of family business problems, such as foreign expansion, internal change,

---

[60] Anonymous, 1994; Lank, 1996
[61] Donckels & Froehlich, 1991; Donckels & Fröhlich, 1991
[62] Donckels, 1996a; Donckels, 1996b
[63] Fröhlich, 1992; Fröhlich, 1995
[64] Watkins, 1996

planning, and banking from countries including Chile, Spain, Mexico, Germany.[65]

In another study Ballarini and Keese looked at the specific characteristics of small family businesses in the southern part of Germany. They found that the average family firm employs 20 people and they also gained other demographic information pertaining to age, level of education, etc.[66].

The analyses of Wimmer et al. and Domayer and Vater led each to conclude that the family business form is both a liability as well as an opportunity, in regards to the future. The successful firms, they conclude, will be the ones that learned the correct way to deal with the risk factors.[67]

Hinterhuber et al. contemplated the medium-sized German family firm and concluded that the family firms are a decisive element in shaping the competitive nature of the economy. Furthermore, they propose the division of family business into the subsystems of family and firm. They suggest that despite the earlier perception of the family as a disturbing factor, harmony between the two systems is necessary to attain sound strategic leadership.[68]

In a number of popular press articles, various authors explore issues of relevance to family firms such as existence threatening factors, the intricacies of dealing with and being part of a family dynasty, prejudicial treatment, the design of a top management organization structure, ownership strategies, and the need for assessing the balance between family and firm.[69]

Löwe reconfirmed the importance of the family business for the economy, and suggested that the best chance for a strategic re-orientation or implementation of new strategies is during the time of generational transfer[70].

---

[65] Ward & Mendoza, 1994

[66] Ballarini & Keese, 1995

[67] Domayer & Vater, 1994; Wimmer, Domayer, Oswald & Vater, 1996

[68] Hinterhuber, Rechenauer & Stumpf, 1994

[69] Kircherer, 1997; Klughardt & Stöhlker, 1994; Ladner, 1996; Pohlschröder, 1990; Wagner, 1994; Widmer, 1995; Zimmerer, 1991

[70] Löwe, 1979

Pine provides detailed guidance on how to make the transition from an entrepreneurial company to a family firm, i.e. steps necessary to successfully involve the second generation family in the firm[71].

Rosenbauer examined the family business through a life-cycle lens and subsequently set forth to determine the strategic competencies necessary for survival[72]. Schmoll determined that the success of the family firm is the union between the owner and its chief executive, as well as the manageable number of employees[73].

Von Schultzendorff analyzed the interplay between non-family managers and family members. He assessed that a number of problems are not communicated and resolved at all, leading to an impasse, as well as the often lacking practical knowledge of management among family members.[74]

2.1.5 Entrepreneurship links

As mentioned in the definition section, a number of parallels between the field of family business and entrepreneurship emerge. Both fields are rather young, have little theoretical structure and attract a variety of people from divergent backgrounds.

Although family business has been categorized as a sub-discipline of entrepreneurship, it seems more correct to state that there are a number of issues that overlap (e.g. often enough entrepreneurs happen to be family business owners as well), and that some researchers based in entrepreneurship have ventured out into family business research. Hence, some efforts are made to point out the links between entrepreneurship and family business.

In an earlier commentary, Brockhaus suggested that the family business field could advance a great deal by avoiding the mistakes made throughout the evolution of the entrepreneurship field in the past 20 years. He particularly pointed to early pitfalls caused by weak measurement instruments, the lack of comparative and longitudinal studies, and generally

---

[71] Pine, 1992

[72] Rosenbauer, 1994

[73] Schmoll, 1986

[74] von Schultzendorff, 1984

underdeveloped research methodologies. Furthermore, the relevance of issues researched was often questionable and the problem of defining entrepreneurship consumed a vast degree of the research debate, but led essentially nowhere. A number of suggestions for future research directions were spelled out.[75]

While the intention of the Brockhaus study was to show the lessons family business could learn from entrepreneurship, Dyer and Handler emphasize the connections between the two fields. Their initial assumption is that entrepreneurship mostly concerned itself with who is an entrepreneur and what it takes to start a successful venture, while family business does not become an issue until the firm is ready to be handed over. Though the analogy of entrepreneurship and family business operating at the opposite ends of the life cycle tends to be a bit oversimplistic, it serves well to point out where the possible connections between the two fields could be. The article proceeds to identify four intersection points of family and entrepreneurial dynamics, namely:

- early experience in the entrepreneur's family,
- family involvement in the start-up activities,
- employment of family members, and
- family involvement in ownership and management succession.

They suggest that these connections and links can further help examine the relationship between entrepreneurship and family business.[76]

Fiol and Aldrich examine the connection between the family and the firm in more general terms. They suggested the two aspects might be united via network theory, but also offered the more abstract insight that the replacement of the family aspect in the venture through professional management cannot solve all inherent problems, rather, family and business must cooperate.[77] Birley struggles with the same problem of interconnectedness between the family and business, but is less positive in her view of the necessary interdependence between the two systems.[78]

---

[75] Brockhaus, 1994a; Brockhaus, 1994b; Brockhaus, 1994c

[76] Dyer & Handler, 1994

[77] Fiol & Aldrich, 1995

[78] Birley & Sorensen, 1995

Lastly, Hoy and Verser explore the boundaries of family business and entrepreneurship by reiterating that both fields constitute a separate domain, with some overlap between the two. They chose to elaborate on the similarities and differences between the two domains, by using six issues from strategic management. And in a last step they use the eight dimensions of entrepreneurship suggested by Gartner, to more specifically outline the commonalties. They pose possible future research questions, which are derived from the eight entrepreneurship themes.[79]

2.1.6 Strategy

A number of studies have explored how family firms deal with strategic management, either to study potential strategic gains to family firms through their organizational form, or to compare family firm studies with entrepreneurship studies (which have found that entrepreneurs are mainly concerned with day to day activities, rather than strategic issues)[80].

This section will discuss recent issues and developments in strategic management and examine their applicability to the family firm. For example, Melin and Hellgren proposed two new change typologies for strategic processes. They reasoned that the existing strategy literature is too often short-term-oriented and a more long-term view must be taken. They propose an approach that combines an entrepreneurial vision with a (long term) strategic mindset, which could constitute a decent fit for family business.[81]

Wortman extended his earlier typological work in entrepreneurship and strategic management to develop a typology of family business strategy. Based on his extensive review of family business studies, he recommends that the field increase its single focus on succession to a broader range of topics, particularly by exploring strategic management and its inherent and suggested issues. This recommendation would quickly advance the field of family business by replicating or validating many of the studies conducted in mainstream strategic management research, such as comparative studies

---

[79] Hoy & Verser, 1994

[80] cf. Martinez & Jimenez, 1995; Swinth & Vinton, 1993

[81] Melin & Hellgren, 1994

of the results of strategic process implementation in publicly held firms to family firms.[82]

In his study of strategic management and family business, Hoy delineates the necessity for firms to engage in strategic action. He finds that large elements of the family business literature are based on strategic management concepts, particularly many of the succession studies. His suggestion for further advancement is an emphasized effort and focus towards strategic issue management in family firms.[83]

In their studies Harris et al. and Ward examined the difference in strategy conception for the family-owned business and non-family-owned firms. They found that large parts of the strategic management formulation and implementation processes are similar for both classes. However, a number of family business characteristics do differ and subsequently affect strategy processes. They identify the following (exemplary) important characteristics:

- inward family orientation and harmony,
- less aggressive growth strategy,
- long term commitment, and
- employee loyalty and care.

They suggest that many of these questions may be resolved through database building, extensive case history analysis, and longitudinal studies.[84]

In 1997 Pramodita Sharma et al. provided a review study of strategic management applications in the family business area. From their extensive review of research studies they describe what is needed to conceive of prescriptive (rather than the existing descriptive) family business studies from a purely strategic management perspective. Based on the 1992 Tagiuri/Davis study Sharma et al. though concede that "prescriptive statements about how family businesses should be managed can only be attempted when the goals/objectives of the family business are identified and considered" (p.7). Their assumed goal of prescription is the advancement of management practice and organisational performance.

---

[82] Wortman, 1995

[83] Hoy, 1995

[84] Harris, Martinez & Ward, 1994; Ward, 1986; Ward, 1995

As with many of the issues surrounding family business, the analysis of the strategic management connections produced more questions than answers. Some concerted systematic efforts are promising, but others constitute mere piecemeal attempts, and offer dubious, if any, contributions.

Related to the topic of strategy is the issue of corporate governance, which has arisen during the past 10 years as one area of mainstream organizational research (cf. multiple journal special issues). Therefore, the book by Neubauer and Lank (1998) provides a long due framework for guidance on how to establish governance structures within family firms.

2.1.7 Organizational behavior

Much like the previous section on strategy, this review attempts to discuss possible domain overlaps and inter-connections between organizational behavior and family business.

Dyer's article on the potential contributions of organizational behavior to the study of family business proposes that the plentifulness of applicable and available theories in organizational behavior should substantially be of assistance in the family business field's needed effort to provide good and sound theories. Dyer's study establishes four levels of analysis from which the potential contributions may be examined: the individual, interpersonal, group, and organization level.

On the individual level he proposes the applicability of the behavioral theories dealing with leadership styles, personal attributes, motivation and career development. Interpersonal-level theories of relevance are communications, role ambiguity, power and influence, and conflict theories. In the group category, theories of group formation and development, group processes, and intergroup conflict could be pertinent. Lastly, on the organizational level, issues of strategic planning, structure and design, culture and governance are applicable.[85]

In a more clinical study, Walsh assesses similar needs for the development of theories overlapping between the behavioral and the family business field. In particular, she identifies the domains of organizational patterns,

---

[85] Dyer, 1994

communication processes, and multigenerational life cycles and belief systems as uniquely posited to provide a complete systems understanding of the family business, provided the theories are further advanced and applied.[86]

2.1.8 Questions unanswered...

This detailed review of the family business literature has made a number of shortcomings explicit. This particular section will strive to comprehensively articulate future research questions, directly resulting from these past shortcomings[87].

A number of issues have prevailed throughout the literature review and should preferably be addressed first:

1. lack of a holistic, systemic theory,
2. lack of depth in research methodologies
3. lack of definitional agreement, and
4. lack of broader scope and approaches.

As became evident through the review of literature dealing with possible contributions and connections between other research streams and family business, no general theory of family business has been established. The last mainstream attempt for a family business theory was presented by Gersick et al. (1997). Based on their collaboration with Caterpillar of over 10 years, they provide a developmental model for understanding and managing patterns of change in family firms. This prescriptive model is based on the existing three dimensions of the business axis, the family axis and the ownership axis. In the end, they develop four classic family business types, namely a) the founder and entrepreneurial experience, b) the growing and evolving family business, c) the complex family enterprise, and d) the diversity of successions: different dreams and challenges. It is noteworthy that they find their theorizing based on the research areas of entrepreneurship, organizational change, networks and succession.

---

[86] Walsh, 1994

[87] in addition cf. Ward, 1997, Dyer/Sanchez, 1998 and Aronoff, 1998 for their (broader) take on the future of the family business field

Other past attempts were generally impartial in nature, as exemplified by Dreux's[88] focus on finance, Davis and Stern's[89] focal point on transition between life cycle stages, and Churchill and Hatten's[90] foundation in succession. Dyer's suggestion to utilize well developed theories from other disciplines should be taken very seriously[91]. Most recently Upton and Heck called for a comprehensive framework, and more systematic theorizing; they in particular called for an integrative family business model from which further exploratory research could then proceed[92]. This current research attempts to provide exactly such a model.

The lack of stringent research methodologies is another deficit Brockhaus, Handler and Wortman rightfully pointed out[93]. This issue was also an initial hindrance for greater advances in entrepreneurship[94], and thus requires of the coming generation of family business researchers not only an openness to a variety of methods and methodologies, but also the training to carry out such research.

The lack of definitional agreement would on the surface suggest a major roadblock to any scientific progress and paradigm unity. However, it seems more important to pursue a better understanding of the processes and motivations underlying family business behavior and of the evolution of this organizational form, than to reach agreement on a static notion. Clearly, a unified definition would be preferable for comparative studies, but this seems unlikely at the current time. One faction of family business scholars is trying to create a very complex definition[95], while the other is aiming towards a simple but inclusive definition[96]. Naturally, the more complex

---

[88] Dreux IV, 1990

[89] Davis & Stern, 1988

[90] Churchill & Hatten, 1987

[91] Dyer, 1994

[92] Upton & Heck, 1997

[93] Brockhaus, 1994a; Handler, 1989; Wortman, 1995

[94] Wortman, 1986; Wortman, 1987; Wortman & Birkenholz, 1990

[95] Litz, 1995

[96] Lank, 1996

definition can accommodate divergent dimensions – at the price of exclusion. For example, any sort of complex definition will ultimately fail in an international context, for the different institutional rules and boundaries will rarely satisfy a complex multi-faceted definition. Hence, more seems to be gained by a simple, inclusive, yet relatively encompassing definition. However, even if a simple definition can be formulated and agreed on, the problem will have merely been shifted towards the operationalization level; and although operationalization is also a problem, it is preferable to a more conceptual disagreement.

For a field born out of integrative, multi-disciplined aspects family business's lack of integration of diverse approaches is surprising. For the field to advance, not only will people from divergent backgrounds need to cooperate, but manifold theories will need to be integrated for the sake of a holistic understanding[97].

2.2 Grounded theory

The literature review on grounded theory attempts to show the development of this methodological path since its inception in 1967. No particular reference to the application of grounded theory to any specific research field will be made; rather, the focus of this review will be on the advancements and refinements the methodology has developed since it began 30 years ago.

Furthermore, the methodology's position in epistemological and also ontological terms will be exhibited.

2.2.1 Basic considerations

As was briefly mentioned before, the grounded theory research methodology is considered a qualitative approach, and while at a later point discourse about the sensibility of the qualitative vs. quantitative dichotomy will be detailed, at this point the definitional rationale of qualitative research by the theory founders shall be delineated.

---

[97] see also Litz, 1997 on why family business research has not been a primary issue on the research agenda of business schools

In their 1967 book, Glaser and Strauss did not explicitly elaborate on definitions of qualitative or quantitative research[98]. They were more concerned with the theoretical implications of what quantitative research stood for and implied, as their argument on the connection of quantitative research with verification nicely reveals[99].

Clearly, their distinction was not between quantitative and qualitative *research* but between quantitative and qualitative *methods*. Subsequently the argument for qualitative research, was an argument for the superiority of qualitative methods in theorizing[100].

Because of the preoccupation with methods, not even necessarily methodologies, not much definite conceptual thought about the implications of grounded theory for epistemology, let alone ontology, had been articulated by 1967.

However, this ostensibly puzzling fact is less ambiguous, given the historical context, namely that positivism was the prevailing paradigmatic stance held in the scientific community.

As competing paradigmatic schools of thought have evolved over the past 30 years (which Guba somewhat arbitrarily clustered and categorized as positivism, post-positivism, critical theory, and constructivism[101]), grounded theory has become more explicit on what it means by qualitative research.

Strauss and Corbin in 1990 posit their definition of qualitative research as follows. "By the term *qualitative research* we mean any kind of research that produces findings not arrived at by means of statistical procedures.... It can refer to research about persons' ... behavior, but also about organizational functioning..."[102]. And while this definition is explicit, it is by no means limiting, or very articulate about what it is not.

---

[98] Glaser & Strauss, 1967
[99] Glaser & Strauss, 1967:185
[100] Glaser & Strauss, 1967:15-18
[101] Guba, 1990:17-27
[102] Strauss & Corbin, 1990:17

Once again, absolute or clear association with a certain research paradigm is not established. Strauss and Corbin continue by outlining the rationale for engaging in qualitative research without being expressly confining. According to them, determinants for using qualitative research should be experience, discipline, philosophical orientations and the nature of the research problem[103].

To infer grounded theory's position on the philosophy of science – given the lack of explicit statements on the issue – conclusions must be drawn from other instances in grounded theory.

Through grounded theory's theorizing from data, and the subsequent immersion of new theories via every study conducted under grounded theory's assumptions, not only is the existence of multiple theories permissible, but furthermore, competing multiple theories are conceivable. With this possibility of manifold rival theoretical conjectures, a positivistic or post-positivistic paradigm – implying the existence of only one objective truth[104] – cannot be attributed to grounded theory.

Subsequently, grounded theory's prescription to a (social) constructivist viewpoint on philosophy of science may be presumed.

Admittedly, what grounded theory considers a new theory, that is, a new theory is created through every grounded theory study, may not be considered a full or grand theory in explanation of a complex reality by all disciplines. However, as the intention of this research is not to define what (or what not) constitutes a theory, the somewhat frail argument and assumption presented for grounded theory's foundation in a (social) constructivist paradigm may be acceptable.

Concluding the iterations on the basic considerations of grounded theory, it can be stated that through the apparent absence of epistemological and ontological positions taken (as well in 1967 as in 1990[105]), no evolving methodological development can be shown for grounded theory.

---

[103] Strauss & Corbin, 1990:19

[104] Guba, 1990

[105] cf. Glaser & Strauss, 1967; Strauss & Corbin, 1990

Grounded theory may be classified in the (social) constructivist paradigm only inferentially. For some critics[106] this reinforces the atheoretical affinity of grounded theory, which should not necessarily be judged, however an awareness of the fact is essential.

Others argue that the purist disposition in extreme paradigmatic positions is a moot point anyhow. Miles and Huberman, for example, state that epistemological views will need to be operationalized at some point, likely necessitating multiple method mixing anyway[107]. Hence, clear *a priori* statement of assumptions becomes their sole concern, a pragmatic, though not necessarily pure solution to the epistemological debate[108].

2.2.2 *Some thoughts on the qualitative/quantitative dichotomy*

Though not central to this research, the question of what really distinguishes qualitative from quantitative research and whether that is even a valid dichotomy is still somewhat relevant.

Some of the debate is fueled by more positivistic oriented researchers, who question the validity of any qualitative research entirely.

Parts of the dilemma were indeed exemplarily displayed through Strauss and Corbin's definition of what qualitative research is[109]. What was not detailed though was what qualitative research is not, nor was quantitative research subsequently defined and how it possibly contrasted with qualitative research.

By the example of one author, the brief argument against the qualitative/quantitative dichotomy will now be exhibited.

Joanne Martin dismisses the qualitative vs. quantitative dichotomy by classifying the methodological arguments as either simple mono-method or complex mono-method approaches[110].

---

[106] cf. Becker, 1993

[107] Miles & Huberman, 1994:4

[108] Miles & Huberman, 1994:5

[109] Strauss & Corbin, 1990:17

[110] Martin, 1990:30

The simple mono-method, for example, would argue that well executed quantitative methods would be inherently superior to qualitative methods. This assertion is then argued to hold across a broad spectrum of organizational research questions[111].

To explain how the justification of such a simple mono method approach is delivered, Martin cites Blau's 1965 critique of the case study approach to organizations[112]. Daft subsequently documented a substantial and steady increase in quantitative papers published in the *Administrative Science Quarterly* journal between 1959-1979[113].

Because then of the usual dominance of such a stance it ordinarily is not stated explicit, rather it remains a tacit assumption, "... the truth of which need not to be explicated to those who are already true believers. It surfaces primarily when newcomers are being indoctrinated (as in some methodology textbooks) and when someone has the temerity to use qualitative methods."[114]

The same example, of course, also holds true for some of the defenses taken up for qualitative research. Arguments are not only about the appropriateness of the chosen method, but also assert their superiority, with some researchers going even further in denigrating quantitative research[115].

After depicting the simple mono-method approach, Martin goes on to illustrate what she classifies as the complex mono-method approach.

In this method the predominance of one approach is explicated out of the complexity of one particular research topic[116]. So in one sense this method's demand on application is not field encompassing, but topic encompassing.

Martin proceeds to challenge both methods in asserting that there is nothing inherent in either method to restrict their usage to particular fields or topics.

---

[111] Martin, 1990:31

[112] Blau, 1965 op.cit. Martin, 1990:32

[113] Daft, 1979 op.cit. Martin, 1990:32

[114] Martin, 1990:32

[115] Martin, 1990:32

[116] Martin, 1990:33-34

Further, whatever method is chosen, trade-offs will be encountered, which can be counter-balanced by method mixing[117].

This method mixing, also called triangulation, in its classical definition contends that different methods are used to come up with the same answer to a single theoretical question. Hybrid models of this method have evolved, and can vary substantially in their divergence from the classical approach to triangulation[118].

In a broad sense then, triangulation allows the researcher to clearly define a theoretical research question and select multiple methods for inquiry according to the research problem[119].

Martin, however, charges that this assumption about the method decision making process might not reflect the empirical reality.

Instead she proposes that Cohen, March and Olsen's "garbage can" model might more accurately reflect the sequence of the method decision making process, because it would suggest that the method choice is driven by the availability of resources, preference or limited skills, and the likelihood that particular results may be found. Additionally, to consciously be able to opt for a multi-method approach the researcher needs to be trained in multiple methods, which certainly cannot be taken for granted in most cases, most of the time[120].

In conclusion, Martin clearly opts for the break-up of methodological monopolies, paired with a plea to fellow researchers to exercise methodological tolerance, if not multi-method mastering[121,122].

---

[117] Martin, 1990:38

[118] Martin, 1990:40-41

[119] for an exemplary application of multi-method mixing cf. Larsson, 1993

[120] Martin, 1990:41

[121] Martin, 1990:42-43

[122] European researchers, when not dismissed as eclectic, have been known to be somewhat more tolerant of multiple methods; for an exemplary insight in some of the more current methods used in research cf. Elfring et al., 1995

2.2.3 Grounded theory in contrast to other methodological approaches

While the first section on grounded theory elaborated on the methodologies evolution and (implicit) epistemological stances, the previous section shed some light on the qualitative vs. quantitative methods discussion from a more abstract philosophical point of view. By all means it helped clarify a) why quantitative vs. qualitative methods is a false dichotomy, and b) what the implicit beliefs and assumptions were, when researchers were taking single or complex mono-methods positions.

In this section some of the more recent methodological debates and the subsequent array of method choices will be reviewed and discussed.

2.2.3.1 The inherent characteristics of qualitative research

This section is set out to discuss in a summary fashion the value of a qualitative research approach, despite the previous elaborations on an argument stating that the labels qualitative vs. quantitative are the seemingly wrong labels.

And although the dichotomy between qualitative and quantitative research is suspect, the realities of the methodology landscape certainly are a) slow to change, and b) hardly modifiable *ex post*. That is to say, to show the value of qualitative research methods one cannot circumvent the usage of this label in the past. And using the label and condoning or justifying it certainly do not necessarily go together.

By using the qualitative methodology of grounded theory, the following advantages are inherent to the approach.
Strauss and Corbin posit that a qualitative approach is particularly appropriate if the research topic is phenomenological in nature and/or if very little is known about the phenomenon[123].

Miles and Huberman further differentiate on the strengths of qualitative data, emphasizing that the approach "*...focus(es) on naturally occurring, ordinary events in natural settings,...*"[124]. The confidence in the method is

---

[123] Strauss & Corbin, 1990:19

[124] Miles & Huberman, 1994:10 italics are as in the original

enhanced by "local groundedness", the fact that the data were collected in proximity to a natural, specific situation. By focusing on the case and its underlying phenomenon, the local context is retained in addition to the greater likelihood that latent, non-obvious issues might surface.[125]

Furthermore, the data's richness and holism, with the potential of revealing complexity, are also important.

If the data are also collected over a period of time, process studies may be conducted, which could go as far as assessing causality. Also, qualitative studies usually are quite flexible in nature.

Lastly, Miles and Huberman allude to the advantage of the qualitative approach in developing hypotheses (in new areas), testing hypotheses, and supplementing quantitative data, when gathered from the same setting[126].

Martin submits as a possible disadvantage to a qualitative approach the fact that it is hard to disentangle confounding variables. Furthermore it is almost impossible to establish causal relationships, due to the complexity and richness of the data. Thirdly, it is rarely possible to install control mechanisms or comparison groups. And lastly, it is almost never possible to develop an abstract and generalizable theory from qualitative data.[127]

2.2.3.2 The benefits of grounded theory

Grounded theory as a general methodological approach, its attributes as part of the qualitative research paradigm, in addition to some other issues, notably the development and epistemology debate, were all discussed at length earlier in chapter two[128].

Having previously established a detailed background for grounded theory, it is for this reason that the detailed benefits of grounded theory will not be elaborated on here, but rather will be portrayed in detail in the methodology

---

[125] Eisenhardt 1989, Glaser & Strauss 1967, and Miles & Huberman 1994:10 all stress this intimate connection with the empirical reality as a major benefit of qualitative research

[126] Miles & Huberman, 1994:10

[127] Martin, 1990

[128] cf. section 2.2 on page 29

chapter[129], which will deal with the methodology choice and the encircling issues.

2.2.3.3 *Triangulation*

The use of the word triangulation occurred earlier in chapter two, when Joanne Martin, in drawing her synthesis against the false argument of the qualitative vs. quantitative dichotomy, propagated the utilization of triangulation to overcome mono method approaches to research[130].

The classical definition of triangulation of Fiske and Campbell suggests that a successful triangulation study is such which uses different methods to come up with the same answer to a single theoretical question[131].
Clearly, since then has the word triangulation been used to describe more varying and inclusive approaches to process mixing.

Triangulation has further been used to describe the mixing of methods, the mixing of data sources, the mixing of theories and perspectives, and the mixing of quantitative and qualitative approaches within a study[132]. A more detailed and excellent discussion of triangulation is provided by Denzin[133]. A more contemporary debate is articulated in the Denzin and Lincoln 'Handbook on Qualitative Research'[134].

A last discussion to be introduced is from Miles and Huberman. Their essential definition states, that "...triangulation is supposed to support a finding by showing that independent measures of it agree with it..."[135]. Their expectation of triangulation is one of corroboration, comparing it to a confidence interval in statistics.

---

[129] cf. section 3 on page 67

[130] Martin, 1990

[131] Fiske and Campbell, 1959 op.cit. Martin, 1990

[132] for an exemplary application of the latter in entrepreneurship research cf. Van de Ven 1992, and in general management research cf. Larsson 1993

[133] Denzin, 1978

[134] Denzin & Lincoln, 1994

[135] Miles & Huberman, 1994:266

This notion of confidence interval can be transcribed into evaluation criteria, i.e. a way of authenticating the outcome of the qualitative research. Guba and Lincoln suggest the following criteria of credibility, transferability, dependability and confirmability as an alternative to the positivistic validity, reliability and objectivity[136]. Similar criterion are echoed by Martin[137]. A more complete discussion on these measures of legitimation are to follow in the methodology chapter.

The point of introducing the notion of triangulation was not to contrast the academic debate and development on the issue. Rather the intention was to provide the reader with a general notion of method mixing, its underlying rationale, and its acceptance/seriousness in the academic debate, as evident through numerous (cited) scholarly publications.

This implies that a) the methodological category of triangulation, and b) the legitimacy of triangulation can be used to justify and defend the mixing of grounded theory with organizational ecology, at least on a formal methodological level.
In later parts, iterations on this interface will focus on the legitimation of triangulation from a philosophy of science point of view, and from a research question-driven legitimation position of the method mixing.

2.2.3.4 The use of cases and case studies

The last topic deserving attention in the discussion surrounding grounded theory is that of cases and case studies (single and multiple).
The intention of the discussion here is to examine the value of the case vs. the case study approach, adding a second dimension through the possible multiplicity of cases or case studies, respectively. The categorical four possibilities are detailed in the matrix below (Figure 3).

---

[136] Guba & Lincoln, 1994
[137] Martin, 1990

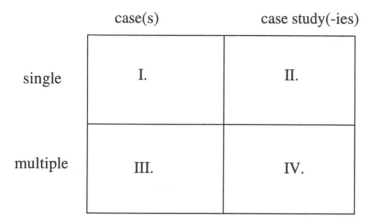

	case(s)	case study(-ies)
single	I.	II.
multiple	III.	IV.

Figure 3: Case Matrix

All four possibilities (quadrants I. - IV.) could be envisioned in the context of a grounded theory study (at least in general terms). The limitation to four categories is voluntary and purist (in the sense of a mono-method) at the same time. It is voluntary insofar as grounded theory permits for many further possibilities of inquiry (not even explicitly delineated by Glaser and Strauss, and Strauss and Corbin), however, due to the focus on actual family businesses a confinement to family business cases seemed sensible. Or put differently, the aggregation and clustering of the data units and pieces seemed most appropriate along the lines of its natural organizational form.

Distinctions between a case and a case study are somewhat arbitrary in that there are hardly any generally agreed upon criteria on what constitutes a case and/or a case study, although guidelines for rigor and other formal measures appear to be emerging.

Both instances of inquiry start with research questions concerning the how and why. The very specific on how to segregate the case from the case study, however, is drawn from the theoretical assumptions.
As Robert Yin notes "... theory development *prior* to the collection of any case study data is (an) essential..."[138]. This is in absolute contrast to the

---

[138] Yin, 1989:36 italics added by this author

39

grounded theory methodology which attempts to carry out research without pre-conceived notions, and developing theory from the data, hence the grounded theory expression, *theorizing from data*[139].

On these theoretical grounds of *a priori* assumptions, i.e. deductive (case study) vs. inductive reasoning (grounded theory[140]), cases and case studies can be logically separated.

Now that it is clear that no case studies (at least in Yin's usage and definition of the term) will find applicability in this study, what then exactly defines a case?

A case embodies data consolidated in the context of the organizational form of the family business. That can entail the selection of a family business according to some general parameter. Upon the selection, publicly available information is collected. The main data, however, will come from interviews conducted within the family business. The number and length of interviews may vary, with the visits to the company limited to one, thereby eliminating a longitudinal process study. A general research strategy is prepared, but no catalogue of questions is submitted.

In summary, the core of the case(s) will be interviews, the outcome of which (data) is collected.

A detailed description on the exact procedures, case selection, and data collection will be provided in the methodology chapter[141].

Once again, the definition of 'case' is arbitrary, however, necessary for distinguishing methodologies. On formal terms, the definition 'case' in some instances resembles that of 'case study', but certainly not on theoretical grounds. The exact justification for this definition will emerge in the methodology chapter.

---

[139] Glaser & Strauss, 1967; Strauss & Corbin, 1990

[140] it should be noted that the grounded theory methodology is inductive as well as deductive; as a theory emerges from the first case it is tested against existing literature, and then more importantly it is tested in the next case, suggesting that the grounded theory is an iterative inductive-deductive-inductive approach.

[141] cf. section 3 found on page 67

After the distinction of case vs. case study, it is now necessary to discuss the possible advantages/disadvantages of a single case as compared to multiple cases.

Eisenhardt recently suggested the general use and appropriateness of case research on the newer frontiers of management research and also elaborated on the utility of multiple cases to build stronger theory[142].

As a result of this article, a dispute between Eisenhardt and Dyer and Wilkins arose, centering around the issue of single vs. multiple cases.

Dyer and Wilkins argued that single cases would be the better stories in that the theory derived from them would be richer and more coherent; in essence their argument becomes one for better stories, not better constructs[143].

Eisenhardt responded by suggesting that the dichotomy 'better stories' (single case) vs. 'better construct' (multiple case) is a false one, since it will be almost impossible to historically substantiate whether certain single cases contributed more, or had greater theoretical insights and impacts, than did certain other multiple cases.

The argument for multiple cases then is specified by arguing that great theoretical insights are achieved through methodological rigor and multi-case comparative logic[144].[145]

With these elaborations on the comparative logic favoring multiple cases, this section on contrasting grounded theory to other methodologies will close.

2.2.4 The hard core vs. the periphery

Chapter one explained that – amongst other factors – organizational ecology was taken into account for this research study because in its recent past the research program started dealing with the issue of organizational core and periphery.

---

[142] Eisenhardt, 1989

[143] Dyer & Wilkins, 1991

[144] a technique which Glaser & Strauss call the 'Constant Comparative' method 1967:101-115

[145] Eisenhardt, 1991

Furthermore, the organizational core was mentioned as a possible and categorically non-deniable recurring variable in the field research process. Based on these two occurrences it was deemed worthwhile to more diligently review the aforementioned concept of hard core and periphery.

The theory of organizational ecology – as propagated by Hannan and Freeman – makes a first explicit listing of the hard core in 1989[146]. The four hard core characteristics mentioned are:

1. stated goals
2. forms of authority
3. core technology, and
4. marketing strategy.

These four core organizational features, as stated by Hannan and Freeman, are at no point explained or derived from any particular inductive or deductive reasoning.

They do, however, constitute a valid starting point and base for later empirical corroborations or refutations.

The latest output from organizational ecologists on the issue of organizational core is from Ginsberg and Baum. They do, however, fail to test or elaborate on the four core categories suggested by Hannan and Freeman. Rather, they employ the more popular definition of organizational core in the context of business growth, i.e. the core business is the initial domain of a firm's activity, while growth facilitates horizontal and vertical acquisitions or new ventures, and thus changes and extensions to the core business incur. This definition is in essence a derivation of terms from strategic management.[147]

Besides organizational ecology, other research programs have taken up the notion of hard core vs. periphery and have explored the possible application and implied benefits of stringent research methodologies, such as the ones proposed by Lakatos or Popper. One example of such application – or at

---

[146] Hannan & Freeman, 1989:79-80
[147] Ginsberg & Baum, 1994

least debate thereof – is in the field of economics. A discussion on the feasibility of Popperian and/or Lakatosian methodologies in economics is provided by Hands[148].

Also indicated earlier in chapter one was the fact that the whole concept of hard core and periphery was not invented by Hannan and Freeman, rather the contemporary philosopher of science Imre Lakatos, introduced the notion[149].

In his delineation of what constitutes a research program, Lakatos asserts that such a program must consist of methodological rules, which "... tell us what paths of research to avoid (*negative heuristics*), and others what paths to pursue (*positive heuristics*)."[150]

The negative heuristic of a research program is also called the hard core. This hard core is irrefutable and hence 'off-limits' for the researcher, instead, a protective belt must be formed around it, which in due course is to be tested and adjusted, affording the core to be even more hardened[151]. These adjustments in turn are to constitute consistently progressive theoretical shifts. If the demand of these consistent shifts is content increasing, Lakatos terms them a 'consistently progressive theoretical problemshift', which now and then ought to be seen as retrospectively corroborated[152].

The reader should be aware that Lakatos did not think of the actual hard core as emerging 'fully armed', which implied that he thought of the process to be a slow, long and preliminary process of trial and error[153].

This hard core, which contains the unquestioned 'essence' of the research program (or paradigm in Kuhnian terms), may not be refuted as long as the corroborated empirical content of the protective belt increases.

However, if the research program ceases to anticipate novel facts, its hard core might have to be abandoned out of logical and empirical reasoning[154].

---

[148] Hands, 1993

[149] Lakatos & Musgrave, 1970

[150] Lakatos, 1978:132 *italics* by Lakatos

[151] Lakatos, 1970

[152] Lakatos, 1978

[153] Lakatos & Musgrave, 1970

The positive heuristic, or also called the protective belt, consists of some articulated sets of suggestions on how to change or develop the refutable variants of the research program, and subsequently refine the refutable protective belt[155].

In essence Lakatos provides for anomalies to the research program, which can be dealt with through the protective belt. Or in Lakatos' own metaphor, the positive heuristic saves the scientist from becoming confused by the ocean of anomalies[156].

In Lakatos' opinion nothing but the existence and utilization of models better proves the necessity for the protective belt better. A model then is a set of initial conditions, possibly paired with observational theory, which is expected to be replaced during the further development of the research program. Hence the positive heuristic serves to strategize, predict and digest refutations (or anomalies)[157].

The two key points to be summarized from Lakatos are a) the advancement of science through verification (rather than falsification), and corroboration of conjectures in the protective belt, and b) a research program, specifically its hard core, can never be refuted, but can only be abandoned when there is an evident lack of consistent empirical content-increasing theoretical problemshifts, a program's failure to anticipate novel facts.

This literature review detailed what the hard core of organizational ecology entails, and more importantly, Lakatos' epistemology and subsequent operationalized assumption of the hard core. His operationalization also provides a clear basis on how to advance and enhance the current organizational ecology core, or what indicators would suggest that the currently existing hard core deserves no further attention and should therefore be abandoned.

---

[154] Lakatos, 1978
[155] Lakatos, 1978:134
[156] Lakatos, 1978:135
[157] Lakatos, 1978:136

Since Lakatos' concept of hard core is proposed for utilization in this research, an explanation of its basic assumptions seemed quite adequate and warranted.

2.2.5 Some more philosophy of science...

The previous section dealt with the notion of hard core, and while reviewing that concept, ample work of Imre Lakatos was utilized.

Acknowledging not only his contribution to the core concept, but moreover recognizing his work in the greater philosophy of science field, competing contemporary accomplishments ought to be equally appreciated.

Without destitution for unnecessary depth, a brief review on the epistemological stances, and the views on the advancement of science of Sir Karl Popper, Thomas Kuhn, and Paul Feyerabend will be provided.

The depiction of Lakatos' view on these issues is deemed sufficient through the detailing of the preceding section.

2.2.5.1 Sir Karl R. Popper

Drawing the inference from Lakatos' view on how a research program is advanced, and also what the criteria for abandonment is, a position for theoretical pluralism – competing research programs – over theoretical monism is taken. In this instance Lakatos is in line with Popper and Feyerabend, but an adversary to Kuhn.

An indication on Popper's view on the advancement of science can be drawn from his 'supreme heuristic rule', which asserts that for a new theory to constitute progress over its predecessor it must be independently testable, must have more empirical content than the predecessor, and must predict novel facts[158]. Nevertheless, as a new theory would emerge and temporarily hold true, it eventually would be falsified, or its ultimate scientific test would be through the provision of probable falsification.

Popper, who can be considered a major contributor to the research program of evolutionary epistemology, has taken the following position on

---

[158] Popper, 1934

epistemology. Popper believed that from natural selection to the growth of scientific knowledge the same principle of trial-and-error-elimination applied. Thus the generalized perspective can always be presumed to entail the following three processes of introduction of variation and novelty, systematic selection among the variants, and preservation or propagation of variants[159]. Indeed, organizational evolutionary theorists with their abstracted basic belief in variation, selection and retention share the same epistemological philosophy as Popper did.

2.2.5.2 Thomas S. Kuhn

What the research program was to Lakatos is the paradigm to Kuhn.

In Kuhn's argumentation any progress is based on what he called 'normal science', which means research firmly based on past achievement, and for the time being is acknowledged by the scientific community[160].

Advancement only comes when continually occurring anomalies lead to a crisis, forcing the scientist to go outside the existing boundaries and explore different explanatory options. This sets the stage for a scientific revolution, which he terms a 'gestalt-switch' and during which a new paradigm emerges. And only at this paradigmatic stage is progress in science possible[161]. Further details, of course, for this sequence of scientific revolution, and paradigm development and acceptance exist, however they would go beyond the need and intention of these somewhat simple and abstracted remarks[162].

At last, it is important to take note of Kuhn's rejection of falsification and his propagation of sequential paradigm development, i.e. theoretical monism through their respective incommensurability[163].

---

[159] Popper, 1985 (Original 1973)

[160] Kuhn, 1970:1-2

[161] Kuhn, 1970:90-91

[162] cf. Kuhn, 1970

[163] further detail on the analysis of Kuhn's argumentation in light of an economics application can be found in Caldwell, 1994

2.2.5.3 Paul K. Feyerabend

In his 'Against Method' book, Feyerabend argues that the existing methodologies of science then current (including all the aforementioned) had failed to provide adequate rules to guide scientists. In the sense that existing methodologies provide for standards, but not rules, Feyerabend argues that subsequently scientists should then not be guided by (these) rules, and hence 'anything goes'[164]. Anything goes, however, is not meant in an unrestricted sense. Anything goes is Feyerabend's proposition for boundary breaking methodologies.

Following this methodological anarchism then is a precondition for progress in science.

Inadequate accounts of past developments, such as logical positivism and falsificationism, are in Feyerabend's opinion liable to hinder progress in science.

Lastly, these deviations from existing methodologies are in his mind not hindrances but pre-conditions for scientific progress, for as Feyerabend put it, because science is much more sloppy and irrational than its methodological images[165].

A mediating concept for these diverging positions is triangulation, which is not as radical as 'anything goes', but is definitely eclectic in its proposition, and certainly a step forward.

Later elaborations will be posited detailing that the *a priori* statement on epistemological beliefs is necessary, but that certain (methodological) boundary breaking (not just spanning) is also necessary, possibly vindicated by the evolutionary variation-selection-retention approach.

The intention of this section on philosophy of science was to give the reader a brief introduction to the positions of Lakatos, Popper, Kuhn and Feyerabend on epistemology and the advancement of science.

---

[164] Feyerabend, 1975:295-296
[165] Feyerabend, 1975:179

For a comprehensive and more detailed treatment and comparison of the main contemporary philosophers of science, the reader is directed toward the work of Alan Chalmers[166].

2.3 Organizational Ecology

This literature review section on organizational ecology will outline the basic assumptions of this research paradigm since its inception in 1977, display what the major research areas have been, and delineate dominant theoretical advances.

The foundational article for what originally was called population ecology, was presented by Hannan and Freeman in 1977[167].[168] The prevalent concern then was to understand vital rates of populations. At that time, organizational-level change was beyond the realm of ecological theory.[169]
Population ecology's main point of divergence from other theories such as institutionalism[170], transaction cost economics[171] and resource dependence theory[172] was that it did not subscribe to the adaptation model of change, but considered organizational change to be the outcome of organizational selection processes.[173]
It also became recognized that methodologies of ecological research required longitudinal data and rate models.[174]
A summary of roughly the first ten years of ecological research can be found in Carroll[175].

---

[166] Chalmers, 1976

[167] Hannan & Freeman, 1977

[168] their work in turn was based largely on and is an extension of the earlier work by Hawley, 1950

[169] Amburgey & Rao, 1996

[170] cf. Meyer & Rowan, 1977; North, 1990; Scott, 1995

[171] cf. Williamson, 1975; Williamson, 1981; Williamson, 1985; Williamson, 1993

[172] cf. Pfeffer & Salancik, 1978

[173] Carroll, 1988

[174] Amburgey & Rao, 1996

[175] Carroll, 1988

The next milestone publication was Hannan and Freeman's 1989 collection of essays entitled 'Organizational Ecology'[176]. As the difference in title (population vs. organizational ecology) reflects, a more refined paradigm had evolved. Not only was the existence of multiple perspectives (individual, organizational, population and community) acknowledged, they even became included as part of the ecological research stream. Perhaps more importantly, while the initial work did not permit for any adaptation to take place, the 'Organizational Ecology' book stated that some adaptation may occur, although it did not specify how.[177]

The next collection of essays, edited by Jitendra Singh in 1990, shifted the field of ecological research from what Carroll had specified as a focus on vital rates[178], to what Singh posited as the investigation on how the environment shapes rates of creation and death of organizational forms, rates of organizational foundings and mortality and rates of change in organizational forms[179]. A further, more substantial difference was the emphasis on a broader theme: organizational evolution.

Finally, another collection of essays appeared in 1994 under the editorship of Joel Baum and Jitendra Singh. The emphasis on broadening the inquiry and applicability of organizational ecology to organizational evolution was restated. Additionally, a more concerted effort was made to further develop and integrate the four divergent levels of analysis, namely intraorganizational, organizational, population and community evolution.[180]

The latest authoritative review of the field and the suggested areas for future research can be found in the latest 'Handbook of Organizational Studies'.[181]

---

[176] Hannan & Freeman, 1989

[177] Hannan & Freeman, 1989

[178] Carroll, 1988:2

[179] Singh, 1990

[180] Baum & Singh, 1994a

[181] Baum, 1996

These introductory paragraphs served to give a historical overview of the evolution of the organizational ecology paradigm and outline the main theoretical advances. The next section will review some of the key achievements in ecological research. Potential shortcomings in the existing research, particularly as they relate to this inquiry, will also be discussed.

2.3.1 Central themes

Following Amburgey and Rao the ensuing main areas of ecological research may be posited as:[182]

- adaptation and selection
- density dependence
- organizational foundings
- organizational mortality.

Before detailing these four specific areas, several central criticisms raised against ecological theory must be discussed.

Perrow criticized ecology's neglect of powerful organizations[183]. This critique has been addressed through the works of Carroll[184], who followed powerful organizations by analyzing size dependence in death rates, Barnett's[185] study of dominance in technological systems, and Amburgey et al.'s[186] analysis of size-based segmentation of populations.

More serious objections were leveled by Young, who pointed to the lack of clear definitions, weak measurements, and narrow focusing on competition[187]. The ecologists, of course, refuted her arguments and asserted that their methods allowed for systematic replication and that there were great benefits derived from broadening the models of competition[188]. The more legitimate discredit of Young's critique, however, came from the

---

[182] Amburgey & Rao, 1996

[183] Perrow, 1986

[184] Carroll, 1984

[185] Barnett & Amburgey, 1990

[186] Amburgey, Dacin & Kelly, 1994

[187] Young, 1988; Young, 1989

[188] Brittain & Wholey, 1989; Freeman & Hannan, 1989

non-ecologist Pfeffer, who reasoned that among the varying organizational research paradigms, ecology carried the highest degree of consensus, had consistency in method-dependent variables, and had recognition of research problems across studies[189].

2.3.1.1 Adaptation and selection

One of the main debates and issues in the organization theory debate over the last few decades is the fundamental question of whether organizations have the ability to adapt to their changing environment – as assumed in the contingency theory of Lawrence and Lorsch[190] – or whether organizations are inherently inert and thus unable to actively change their organizational parameters – as argued by Hannan and Freeman[191] and their followers in the ecology paradigm.

Some more recent ecological research has looked at the effect of organizational links on the rates and effect of change[192] and the effects of change on survival prospects[193].

However, the major theoretical belief remains that even if organizations are able to proactively change, their chances of survival are reduced immensely. A more recent study reviewed works that have contrasted adaptation and selection, and found problems relating to the neglect of the sources and effects of changes, as well as the life chances of the organization – among other matters[194].

An inherent part of the adaptation-selection problem has been that even though some ecological research on adaptation has been legitimately carried out (most visibly in the recent collection of ecology and evolutionary theory essays[195]), its unit of analysis has been the individual agent or the

---

189 Pfeffer, 1993

190 Lawrence & Lorsch, 1967; cf. Thompson, 1967

191 Hannan & Freeman, 1977; Hannan & Freeman, 1984

192 Miner, Amburgey & Stearns, 1990

193 Amburgey, Kelly & Barnett, 1993

194 Barnett & Carroll, 1995

195 cf. parts II + III of Baum, 1994a

organization. Whereas the selection-focused research stayed within the realm of populations and communities.

From these observations it can be concluded that apparently selection forces are hard to observe at the individual or organizational level, while proxies for population or community-level adaptation also do not exist.

This somewhat dilemmatic but empirically real situation can only be rectified through the logical deduction of the interrelation between adaptation and selection. Figure 4 will help illuminate the situation.

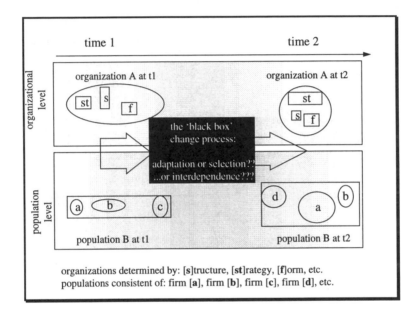

Figure 4: The Adaptation vs. Selection Dilemma

The *assumption* is of any organization or population with given properties which would characterize a 'typical' organization/population, through the specification of elements such as structure, strategy, form, etc. at a given time 1 in a constrained environment A.

At time 2 the same organization/population is revisited and re-assessed, which leads most likely to the determination of certain changed properties, while others will have remained constant. Note the difference in shape, form and elements of organization A and population B at time 1 versus time 2.

If the unit of analysis is the population, the determination of change will be the count of existence (death, transformation, 'old' existence), allowing population dynamics to be observed and established.

If, however, the unit of analysis is the organization, the assessment at time 2 will lead to the determination of the existence of the organization (or death or transformation), while in a second step, change or constancy in organizational parameters and properties can be established. This detailed insight however, is not available from a population observation, however, neither can these organizational insights be considered to be representative of the population development.

Clearly, these are the trade-offs of depth vs. width. The crux, however, with both observations is the assumption of linear and exclusive causality of "the one" change process, which can be proven neither by logic nor by empirical fact.

Plus, the more cumbersome problem is that at time 2 only effects are observed, and even if one accepts the limitation of the causal inference drawn from this one change event, the change event itself cannot be completely observed, and subsequently it will remain unclear whether the change event embodied adaptation, selection or an interdependent selection-adaptation process, since the outcome of both processes is **identical**.

Elaborating on the same issue, Baum in a recent contribution also questioned whether selection and adaptation are really mutually exclusive. He suggested the existence of a complex relationship between selection and adaptation while still maintaining the prevalence of selection forces with supplementing adaptive processes under certain conditions.[196]

2.3.1.2 *Density dependence*

Hannan originally proposed that legitimization and competition instill a U-shaped relationship function between the number of organizations (density) and the failure rate of organizations. So, initial increases in density, i.e. the number of organizations in a population, increases the legitimacy of a population, thereby increasing foundings and lowering failures. But further increases produce competition, suppressing foundings and increasing failures. So, an inverted U-shaped relationship was proposed to underlie

---

[196] Baum, 1996:106

density and the founding rate. For a review of study results supporting this proposition see Hannan and Carroll[197].

However, others have questioned the credibility of density as a proxy for cognitive legitimacy[198]. Remedies in the form of using the concept of mass dependencies, accounting for the variability of influence and impact, were suggested[199]. Further research explored differences in density dependence among death and founding rates. A new approach called relational density was put forward and found divergence in density rates, suggesting a positive value to a relation, resulting in higher founding and lower death rates. A concept of overlap density was also introduced, allowing the effects of competition (and mutualism) to be distinguished from legitimation, the two aspects of density dependence theory underlying population density and organizational founding or disbanding[200].

A fierce debate between Hannan et al. and Baum and Powell has taken place, with the latter arguing for non-density based measurements to account for sociopolitical legitimacy, and Hannan et al. arguing in favor of the parsimonious account of vital rates through density-based approaches to legitimation, while acknowledging though that sociopolitical legitimacy may not be an exogenous variable but rather a consequence of population processes.[201]

A more promising route was suggested by Amburgey and Rao, who pointed to the lack of distinction and research between the legitimation of an organizational form and that of an individual organization. Clearly, issues such as reputation, status and spill-over effects are of influence and need dire attention.[202]

----

[197] Hannan & Carroll, 1992

[198] Zucker, 1989; cf. Zucker, 1988 and Zucker, 1987

[199] Barnett & Amburgey, 1990

[200] Baum & Singh, 1994b; Baum & Singh, 1994c

[201] Baum & Powell, 1995; Hannan & Carroll, 1995; Hannan, Carroll, Dundon & Torres, 1995

[202] Amburgey & Rao, 1996

2.3.1.3 Organizational foundings

Due to the lack of data on pre-organizing activities, most ecological research understates the issue of organizational diversity, since only successful foundings are accounted for. Hence, most pre-start-up micro-processes are not elucidated by ecological theory[203]. For a more detailed review on the ecological analyses of foundings see Aldrich[204].

A nationwide council, called the Entrepreneurship Research Consortium was recently formed by Paul Reynolds of Babson College to further investigate these areas of nascent entrepreneurship, of which so little is known. As the study is just past the pilot phase, no results are available yet.[205]

2.3.1.4 Organizational mortality

The ecology researcher faces a similar dilemma in regards to mortality as one does to foundings. Usually the dearth of detailed data is persistent. Subsequently, one cannot discriminate for disbanding by bankruptcy, merger or absorption. Also, sole reliance has been put on the accuracy of financial performance as the predictor of mortality. In addition, the question remains whether poorly performing organizations fail faster, or persist longer than others.[206]

2.3.1.5 Further categories of ecological research

A more detailed – although certainly overlapping – list of issues in ecological research is provided by Lomi, who identifies the following six topics as core issues of ecological research (citations in footnotes identify key works):[207]

---

[203] cf. Delacroix & Carroll, 1983

[204] Aldrich, 1990; Aldrich & Wiedenmayer, 1993

[205] Selz, 1996

[206] Amburgey & Rao, 1996

[207] Lomi, 1995a

a) density dependent evolution[208]
b) density delay[209]
c) population dynamics[210]
d) resource partitioning[211]
e) community dynamics[212]
f) age dependence[213]

The point of this listing is to not only make the reader aware of additional subgroupings in the ecology research school, but also to provide and direct the reader to exemplary research in the identified sub-area. Neither of these research themes was detailed here at any length, for its strict relevance to this research project was not given. All of these topics specify a detail not called for in this research, in addition to requiring detailed longitudinal data sets of populations.

2.3.2 Questions remaining...

The suggestions below may be considered the emerging issues in ecological research and are listed in completeness for the reader interested in ecology. However, since not all of these issues are of concern and bearing to this particular project, the listing is sub-divided into a category of potentially relevant issues to this research, and a category with the remaining topics. All applicable themes are developed further after the categorical listing. (Citations in footnotes identify key works.)

---

[208] cf. Hannan & Carroll, 1992

[209] cf. Carroll & Hannan, 1990

[210] cf. Delacroix & Carroll, 1983

[211] cf. Carroll, 1985; Freeman & Lomi, 1994

[212] cf. Aldrich, Zimmer, Staber & Beggs, 1994; Barnett & Carroll, 1987; Brittain & Wholey, 1988; Lomi, 1995b

[213] cf. Hannan, 1988

Emerging ecological topics *potentially relevant* to this research:	Emerging ecological topics with *no relevance* to this research:
• entrepreneurship[214]	• computational models[215]
• innovation[216]	• ecology and social networks[217]
• ecology of strategy and change[218]	• ecology of agency arrangements[219]
• adaptation, selection and change[220]	• organizational growth[221]
	• organizational size distributions[222]
	• institutional ecology[223]
	• location dependence[224]

Starting with entrepreneurship, ecology up to now fails to give adequate account of entrepreneurial initiatives. Due to the pre-occupation with rates, no knowledge on the particularities of start-up processes and the variation in forms present then, has been gained or developed.

Also, the research pendulum up to now has swung between traits- and rates-based approaches. Neither has produced more than marginal results, which might suggest the necessity for different progressions.

---

[214] cf. Aldrich & Auster, 1986; Aldrich & Fiol, 1994; Aldrich & Wiedenmayer, 1993; Baum & Singh, 1994b

[215] cf. Lomi & Larsen, 1996

[216] cf. Anderson & Tushman, 1990; Tushman & Anderson, 1986

[217] cf. Burt, 1992

[218] cf. Amburgey et al., 1993

[219] cf. Lynn & Rao, 1995; Nielsen & Rao, 1992

[220] cf. Havemann, 1992; Havemann, 1993; Levinthal, 1995

[221] cf. Haveman, Baum & Keister, 1996

[222] cf. Barnett & Amburgey, 1990; Hannan, Ranger-Moore & Banaszak-Holl, 1990; Winter, 1990

[223] cf. Baum & Oliver, 1996; Baum & Powell, 1995

[224] cf. Baum & Mezias, 1992; Carroll & Wade, 1991; Lomi & Larsen, 1996

The issues of innovation[225] and learning[226], as well as strategy[227] have just recently been legitimately included in the ecological research. And although much integration work lies ahead, the step towards inclusion was an important one[228].

These aforementioned themes as well as that of adaptation and selection will be expanded in the model development section.

2.3.3 The fit of grounded theory and organizational ecology

The purpose of this last review section on grounded theory is to examine the discrepancies between grounded theory and the premises of organizational ecology, i.e., the compatibility of the organizational ecology research program with the grounded theory research methodology in light of the epistemological assumptions in particular.

As was elaborated on earlier, grounded theory's epistemological view can be safely qualified as social constructivist, in that it is built on the assumption of allowance for multiple co-existing theories, implying the social constructivistic stance, in that realities, truth etc. are subjective and based on personal perception.

Organizational ecology on the other hand has through its early focus on populations been mostly concerned with rates-themes (rates of birth, rates of death, rates of transformation, etc.). Subsequently, a strong line of quantitative models and methodologies was employed. This, however, has been changing in the recent past, through the development of ecological research in areas concerning other levels of analysis, such as inter- and intra-organizational levels. With this venturing into extended units of analysis came the multiplicity of methodological advances. These now, in addition

---

[225] cf. Rosenkopf & Tushman, 1994; Van de Ven & Garud, 1994; Van de Ven & Polley, 1992

[226] cf. Mezias & Lant, 1994; Miner, 1994; Miner & Haunschild, 1995; Miner & Robinson, 1994

[227] Barnett & Burgelman, 1996; Fombrun, 1994

[228] for a recent integrative attempt on "organizational evolution" cf. Aldrich, 1999

to longitudinal quantitative approaches, included cases and case studies[229]. Hence, one may speak of internal legitimation of multiple methodologies in ecology. One must, however, be careful about the inferences drawn from this development and the initial methodological viewpoints in ecology. And while no explicit stance on epistemology is articulated, the mere existence of manifold methodological approaches in ecology may serve as a proxy for the permissibility of multiple realities, indicating conformity to a more social constructivist epistemology.

Despite the logical epistemological compatibility of organizational ecology and grounded theory, it is not obvious why grounded theory methodology would go together with ecological theory. Now, without redrawing earlier arguments made in this chapter, refuge for *explanans* may be taken with Feyerabend's 'anything goes'[230] and the discussion on triangulation[231], although Baum's recent suggestion that new ecological research should be question-driven, which may entail the usage of qualitative methods, paints a bright and encouraging future of methodological multiplicity, and at the same time provides legitimation from within the ecology research school[232]. As this study is the first application of ecological conjectures in conjunction with a grounded theory methodology, no other egress is apparent.

2.4 The European Union

The European Union as perceived of for this study signifies the environment and the institutional structure within which the study is presented. The prevalent reason for choosing the European Union as the geopolitical scenario can be attributed to its uniqueness, which is not even rivaled by the North American Free Trade Agreement (NAFTA). The development of the European Union has, does or will affect all family businesses located within its geographical boundaries, as previous borders and restrictions to trade are to diminish and ultimately disappear. This kind of development affecting every firm is unparalleled, and merits particular inquiry.

---

[229] cf. various subsections of Baum, 1994a

[230] cf. section 2.2.5.3 on page 47

[231] cf. section 2.2.3.3 on page 37

[232] Baum, 1996:108

The following sections will detail the evolution of what is now known as the European Union and will also elaborate on the foundations of the Union and the internal processes that underlie it.[233] But first, further deliberations as to the choice of the European Union (EU) as the elected geopolitical setting and institutional frame are to be conveyed.

2.4.1 The institution and process of the European Union

As was mentioned previously, the context chosen for this study is the European Union. In the ensuing parts of this chapter elaborations on the history of the Union, its political evolution, the democratic foundations, and an outlook for the future single market are to be stated.

The implications of choosing such an environment are manifold. For one this is a unique opportunity to observe such a gigantic environment and institutional infrastructure develop and unfold. Through the talks in the cases, it is possible to observe economic agents attempt to make sense of the events. This sense-making process – in the Weickian denotation[234] – provides first-hand insight into how the Maastricht treaty in particular influenced the business lives of the firms. And based on these cognizant processes of past sense-making, inferences and projections to the future could be observed and attained. So in one sense, this allowed the study to maintain a process view – though admittedly a subjective one – while also providing for the possibility of the analysis of contents. This concludes the prospect of the Union as a *process*.

However, another important aspect or conception of the European Union is that of the Union in its *institutional* sense. A whole strand of research on this issue in organizational theory has evolved[235]. In economics a whole branch of research has in particular sprung up and become important since the fall of the 'Berlin Wall' and the 'Iron Curtain'. The demise of the

---

[233] all the information below on history and chronological developments was obtained from documents of the European Union's Information Office, 1996

[234] cf. Weick, 1995

[235] cf. Scott, 1995 for a current approach to the topic; the 'classic' article is Meyer & Rowan, 1977

creation of new institutions and institutional frameworks necessary. The Nobel-laureate Douglas North in particular emphasized the need for a sufficient and well conceived framework that would assure the smooth functioning of the economy through, for example, guarantee of property rights, rightly installed rewards, incentives and castigation.[236]

It is essential to show the importance of the European Union as an environment and institutional structure because of the negative impact and consequences that will follow an ill-conceived or enacted institutional framework. Unlike the countries of eastern Europe, the Union cannot afford the luxury of installing a framework from scratch; rather, it must cope with existing structures and governments, and seek to incorporate these future intentions with current realities. Naturally, compromise will be an important aspect of this process, although sight of the greater goal of the European Union for the satisfaction of current demands must not be lost. If one is to take the example detailed in this chapter[237] outlining how ineffective the current legal system is for businesses to operate in multiple countries, a great many advances are necessary for a smooth and efficient institutional framework to become reality. Presently, it is not the lack of sound ideas or concepts hampering progress, but the harmonization of existing structures with the new setting.

2.4.2 Chronology of the Union

The chronology below[238] provides the complete information on the post World War II Europe pertaining to the European Union.

1947	Marshall plan for the economic revival of a Europe devastated by war
03/1948	Benelux treaty enters into force
1948	Creation of the Organization for European Economic Cooperation (OEEC) to administer the Marshall plan
1949	Creation of the Council of Europe in Strasbourg
05/1950	Schuman Declaration

---

[236] North, 1990

[237] cf. section 2.4.6 on page 65

[238] Information Office, European Union 1996

04/1951	Signing of the Treaty of Paris establishing the European Coal and Steel Community (ECSC)
1952-54	Preparation and failure of the plan for a European Defence Community (EDC)
06/1955	Building of Europe relaunched by the Messina conference
03/1957	Signing of the Treaties of Rome establishing the European Economic Community (EEC) and the European Atomic Energy Community (Euratom)
1967	Merger of the institutions of the three Communities (ECSC, EEC and Euratom)
07/1968	Completion of the customs union
01/1972	Signing of the Treaties of Accession of Denmark, Ireland, Norway and the United Kingdom
01/1973	Denmark, Ireland and the United Kingdom join the European Community
05/1979	Signing of the Treaty of Accession of Greece
06/1979	First election of the European Parliament by direct universal suffrage
01/1981	Greece joins the European Community
06/1985	Signing of the Treaties of Accession of Portugal and Spain
01/1986	Portugal and Spain join the European Community
02/1986 to 07/1987	Signing of the Treaty and entry into force of the Single Act
10/1990	Unification of Germany
02/1992	Signing of the Treaty on European Union ("Maastricht Treaty")
01/1993	Introduction of the single European market and the European Economic Area
11/1993	Coming into force of the "Maastricht Treaty" creating the "European Union"
06/1994	Signing of the Treaties of Accession of Austria, Finland, Norway and Sweden
01/1995	Austria, Finland and Sweden join the European Union

Table 1: Chronology of the European Union

62

2.4.3 The history of the Union

On the 1st of January 1995, Austria, Sweden and Finland joined the European Union. The initial European Economic Community, which started in the 1950's with only six member countries, is now composed of 15 states.

The European Union has a population of 370 million people and its territory stretches from Crete to the arctic circle. The 6 billion ECU gross national product is 10 percent higher than the USA and 64 percent higher than Japan. Currently it is conceivable that by the year 2000, the European Union could grow to more than 25 member states by including central and eastern European countries, as well as Malta and Cyprus.[239]

Figure 5[240] provides a graphical depiction of the development of the European Union.

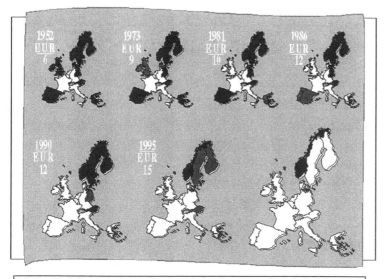

white = Union member; grey = prospect; dark = non-member

Figure 5: The Evolution of the European Union

---

[239] Information Office, European Union 1996
[240] Information Office, European Union 1996

2.4.4 The evolution of the European Union

European integration began in the aftermath of World War II. Founding members of the Community first pooled their heavy industries. They then set about creating a single market in which goods, services, people and capital could move about as freely as within one country. The process was gradual, spanning 40 years and covering political and social as well as economic and trade dimensions. As they completed the single market, which formally came into being in January 1993, the member states also prepared for the future. The Maastricht Treaty on European Union took effect on November 1, 1993. It strengthens the community further, most notably by preparing the way for economic and monetary union (EMU) and a single currency and by giving extra power to the European Parliament. Maastricht also added a common foreign and security policy and cooperation on justice and police affairs. The term 'European Union' is used to describe the wider Maastricht framework in which all these activities take place.[241]

2.4.5 The democratic foundations of the European Union

The European Union is a union of 15 democratic states. Its main institutions are the European Parliament, the European Commission, the European Court of Justice, the Council of Ministers and the Court of Auditors. The Council and the European Parliament are the main decision-making bodies of the EU. The Council consists of ministers from the member states directly responsible to their national governments and parliaments. The 626 members of the European Parliament are elected by EU citizens every five years. The president and the other 19 Members of the European Commission, which has the sole right to initiate draft legislation, are nominated by common agreement by their governments. They are subject to a vote of investigation from the European Parliament before taking office. The parliament also has the right to dismiss the European Commission if it passes a motion to this effect.[242]

---

[241] Information Office, European Union 1996

[242] Information Office, European Union 1996

2.4.6 The single market in 1995

The single market has been at the center of the European Union's development over the last ten years. Its key guarantees – free movement of people, goods, services and capital – are seen as the basis for the future prosperity of the Union and need to be completed by Economic and Monetary Union, scheduled to take place not later than January 1, 1999. However, the single market construction is still not complete, even though progress was made in 1995. The commissioned panel stressed that the legislative program for the single market is still not completed, for example, it is not possible to set up a European company able to operate on the same legal basis in more than one member state because the European Company statute has still not been approved by the Council of Ministers. One authoritative report puts the consequent cost to business at more than ECU 30 billion a year.[243]

2.4.7 Small and medium-sized enterprises in the European Union

Of primary importance to this study in the context of the European Union are the small and medium-sized enterprises.

While initially the European Union defined small and medium-sized enterprises as companies employing between 1 and 500 employees, with micro-enterprises defined at the employment level of 1-9, small firms at 10-49 employees, and medium-sized enterprises at 50-499[244]. The newer definition states that while micro and small firms retain their definition (1-9 and 10-49 respectively), medium-sized enterprises are now defined as firms employing between 50-249 people[245].[246]

In a recently released report by Eurostat (the official EU statistical agency), small and medium-sized enterprises were labeled the backbone of the European Union. Altogether 99% of the firms in the European Union have fewer than 50 workers, and, combined, employ 52 million people. Small

---

[243] Information Office, European Union 1996

[244] cf. SME Observatory, 1994

[245] cf. SME Observatory, 1996:47

[246] further reference to definitional issues can be found on page 73

and medium-sized enterprises provide for two-thirds of all jobs in the European Union, equivalent to 68 million jobs, while accounting for almost 40% of turnover.[247]

2.5 A summary of implications for this research

The intention of this literature review section was to dissect and critically portray the relevant literature from family business, grounded theory and organizational ecology. A final subsection was dedicated to reporting on the evolution of the European Union and the criterion for choosing it as the geopolitical setting of this study.

The family business section gave an overview of the variety of research being carried out. Clearly, family business is by no means as far advanced as, e.g. organizational ecology, and hence more effort had to be spent on basic issues, such as general direction of the field, use of methods, and definitional issues.

The grounded theory section mostly concerned itself with depicting or inferring epistemological stances of this methodology, and critically examining it in contrast to other approaches. Lastly, grounded theory's fit with the stringent organizational ecology framework was discussed.

The section on organizational ecology gave a historical account of the development of the field and critically assessed its advances, as well as its failure to deal with a number of issues.

The coming chapter introduces the reader to the methodology employed in this research.

---

[247] cf. EUROSTAT Enterprises in Europe (4th report), 1996

3. METHODOLOGY

This methodology chapter is divided into four parts. The first part is an introduction into the procedures which will be followed in approaching, selecting and visiting the particular family enterprises. It will include a description of the criteria used, such as industry specifics, firm size, and generational cycles. This part will also give the reasoning behind the choice of countries and the implications of that choice.

The second part is an outline of the guidelines for working with the grounded theory method.

The third part of this chapter is an introduction and description of INTERSTRATOS - the source intended for the validation of results from the initial grounded theory model, along with a description of the statistical techniques used in the analysis.

The fourth and last part of this chapter is an explanation of how the methodology of grounded theory and conjectures from the theory of organizational ecology will be utilized in a family business framework.

Just as Henry Mintzberg's insights served as a foundation for the introductory remarks in chapter one, so here some of Gregory Bateson's observations about epistemology and scientific method can lay a basis for understanding the topics to be discussed in this chapter. In particular, Bateson's insistence on the need for both strict and loose scientific thinking offers legitimation for the attempt in this research project to bring together the more formal theory of organizational ecology with the less strictly scientific approach of grounded theory.

> "(W)henever we start insisting too hard upon 'operationalism' or symbolic logic or any other of these very essential systems of tramlines, we lose something of the ability to think new thoughts. And equally, of course, whenever we rebel against the sterile rigidity of formal thought and exposition and let our ideas run wild, we likewise lose. As I see it, the advances in scientific thought come from a *combination of loose and strict*

thinking, and this combination is the most precious tool of science."[248]

This process of oscillation which Bateson describes can also be termed triangulation.

3.1 Formal description

In this section the reasoning and procedures of the method will be delineated. Because the argument for this particular methodology, along with an outline of its epistemological implications, have been made in the previous chapter, the following descriptions will be rather concrete[249].

3.1.1 The procedure

It is preferable to observe family businesses in a dynamic environment, because a static environment provides no basis for observing processes of change. As has been argued elsewhere[250] the European Union is certainly such a dynamic environment in which family businesses can be observed.

Given the geographical size and extent of the European Union, a number of countries had to be selected. And although the selection satisfies the condition of randomness, the reasoning for the choice of each country can be stated as follows.

Because there was not enough time and money to visit family firms in all the 15 countries of the European Union, only four member states and non-member Switzerland were selected. For reasons to be explained below, these five countries were considered sufficient in number and in differential dynamics to be a legitimate representation of the European Union, therefore allowing this research question to be discussed in the context of the European Union.

---

[248] Bateson, 1972:49; emphasis in original
[249] cf. section 2.3.3 on page 58
[250] cf. section 2.4 on page 59

The European Union countries chosen were (in alphabetical order): Austria, Denmark, Germany and Sweden. Switzerland, though a non-member of the European Union, was also included for reasons to be given below.

Even among these five countries the following differential dynamics can be observed.

First, Denmark and Germany represent the long existing core of the European Union. Second, Austria and Sweden are among the most recent additions to the European Union, although with some previous, weak ties to the European Union countries through their respective memberships in the European Free Trade Agreement (EFTA). Third, Switzerland is a nation with a long and continued absence from the European Union.

It was initially hypothesized that three differences in the factor called relationship to the European Union - namely, long-time membership, recently achieved membership, and lack of membership - would have an observable effect on the behavior of these family businesses, though this could not be operationalized as it later turned out.

After it was determined that these five countries were valid examples of the required dynamic process, the method required that the following operational questions be asked:

1. how many cases ought to be sought within each selected country?
2. what kind of interview format should be used?
3. how many family business members should be interviewed?
4. what other variables ought to be considered and controlled for?

The answer to question number one is in an abstract sense rather simple. The grounded theory methodology subscribes to the notion of theoretical saturation. This means that as the theory or model develops gradually and cumulatively through each new case until, after a certain number of cases, a point will be reached at which no further useful insight is gained from additional cases[251]. Economists describe this general phenomenon as the law of diminishing returns.[252]

---

[251] Glaser & Strauss, 1967:188; Strauss & Corbin, 1990:61-2

[252] Prof. Dr. Pleitner pointed out this pragmatic yet operational method, which the author gratefully acknowledges (personal communication, 1996).

While the abstract rule seems rather simple to follow, empirical realities are rarely so simple. However, since the interview and data collection process took place in clear sequence and extended over a period of six months, the model emerging from the data suggested saturation was reached at a definite point, and after that no further cases were pursued.

The answer to question number two is, for the most part, dictated by the grounded theory methodology and in this instance is supplemented by general guidelines for doing case research. However, other interview methods exist and for the sake of completeness the various general kinds of interviews ought to be mentioned. In the literature a basic distinction between structured, semi-structured and open-ended interviews can be observed[253].

Each category, of course, has its own distinctive characteristics. For this study the semi-structured interviews seemed best suited to guide this research inquiry[254]; the closely structured interview would violate the epistemological assumptions of the chosen grounded theory methodology, while the unstructured interview might be better suited for studies of exploratory nature.

This research closely follows the guidelines provided by Holstein & Gubrium, on how to conduct the active interview[255].

The basic rules and underlying assumptions of the active interview can be established as follows. The interviewer must be prepared to furnish precedence, incitement, restraint and perspective. Furthermore, the introduction should include an implicit request to participate and should strategically convey the topic areas to be explored. And while the active interview is basically a conversation, it is not without a guiding purpose and

---

[253] cf. Miles & Huberman, 1994

[254] the author is indebted to Prof. W. Gibb Dyer, Jr. for illuminating the benefits of semi-structured interviews as opposed to solely unstructured interviews (personal communication, 1995).

[255] Holstein & Gubrium, 1995

plan. To that end, "The Active Interview" provides advice for structuring the interview's agenda.[256]

Inasmuch as grounded theory requires the researcher to maintain a certain level of sensitivity in the field setting[257], the active interview advises the researcher to be familiar with the material, cultural and interpretive circumstances, including a certain vocabulary. In addition, a sound knowledge of such background will allow the researcher to express abstract questions and concerns in concrete terms which are familiar and relevant to the respondents; this concreteness will in turn permit the respondents to answer more meaningfully[258].

In answering question number three an example of the distinction between *a priori* ideal purposes and the necessity for the adjustment of these ideal purposes because of discovered empirical realities will be revealed. *A priori* it seems desirable to conduct interviews with the head of the business, all members of the family involved in the venture, as well as all members of the management team, and also, if possible, board members. The purpose of this inclusive approach is to gain access to the most complete picture possible.

However, this inclusive approach has definite constraints, which can be illustrated by the example of the owner who explicitly states that no one but he himself (she herself) is to be interviewed! One possible explanation for such statements might be generational or intergenerational conflicts.

Additionally, the following constraints are also characteristic when approaching family firms. Comparability across cases cannot be attained since the family business definition and/or the institutional framework do not require of all families, the same degree of involvement in the company. Also, since there is a great likelihood that almost all medium-sized firms are

---

[256] Holstein & Gubrium, 1995:76

[257] Strauss & Corbin, 1990

[258] Holstein & Gubrium, 1995:77

71

closely held and as such are not required by law to have a supervisory board not all of them will have such a board.

Regardless of the various implicit or explicit reasons for the constraints affecting the inclusive approach, it is clear that, if interviews are to be attained (within modest monetary and time limitations), certain concessions need to be made.

Hence, an agreeable but dictated empirical reality is that in most cases, interviews will be confined solely to the current entrepreneur, implying that the only constant across the sample of cases will be the interview with the current chief executive of the company.

An insight from prior research is the fact that the most precise and insightful information for a research question, such as the one in this study, comes from the entrepreneur, the person in charge[259]. This statement is derived from comparative research in instances were multiple interviews were possible. By no means however, is the implication that only entrepreneurs can provide precise and valuable information, but that for the research questions as outlined in this project, the most effective method for attainment of the information coincides to be the most efficient as well. Many other research questions are imaginable in which the entrepreneur might not be the best suited person to be interviewed.

Question number four somewhat functions as a 'catch-all' category. In answering the question, the principal intention is to show awareness of certain issues, which for one reason or another could not be included or dealt with expressly in the empirical study design.

The main issue is that of controlling for certain variables. While this somewhat positivist notion can be dealt with on a theoretical level, in showing that the nature of this study is not quantitative (which would more likely require that sort of controlling), it furthermore becomes clear through the overarching purpose - the purpose of developing a sound model, rather than proving a generalizable factual finding.

---

[259] cf. Hedberg, 1996

However, issues such as industry, firm size, and generational status (life cycle) were considered in the study design.

So as the processes to be studied are those of change, the most likely and most observable place is that of a fast changing industry of concern to family firms. Henceforth, the electronics industry seems like a choice that fulfills that criterion. However, it furthermore is recognizable that with such a catalog of specification (industry, size, generational status), particularly in the smaller countries, the likelihood of even finding such firms are close to zero. As these early intentions for maintaining some categories disintegrate in the study design, a further vital fact though is recognizable. Namely, the fact that most family business owners are not willing to be interviewed if an industry competitor as well is to be interviewed.

Posterior, it is reasoned that the firm ought to have a size which would guarantee that the business would be affected at all by the implications of the European Union, while also assuring that its size was not market-domineering or overpowering. Ensuing, medium-sized companies seem to conform best to that criterion, as particularly smaller companies cannot be assumed to be as substantially affected by the implications of the European Union.

This study will utilize the **definition** of *a medium-sized company being a firm employing between 50 and 249 people*. This definition is currently adopted officially by the European Union. However, at the outset of this study in 1995, the European Union employed the definition of a medium-sized company being one employing between 50 - 499 people. Recently however, the European Union changed its set of definitions, and currently medium-sized companies are defined by the aforestated employee level of 50 - 249.[260]

It may be remarked that all firms involved in this study qualify as medium-sized companies under the "old" and the prevalent standard put in effect by the European Union.

---

[260] cf. SME Observatory, 1996

For an authoritative and encompassing discussion on the issue of defining small or medium-sized enterprises (SME), refer to Mugler[261], who discusses at length the academic debates on the topic. For the purposes of this study the aforestated definition shall suffice.

In concluding the procedure section, two further issues deserve mentioning. For one, in accordance with grounded theory prescription and to provide the most accurate basis for analysis all interviews will be recorded on tape[262]. All interview participants will be requested to give explicit permission to utilize a tape recorder. At the same time, the researcher agrees not to publicize the content of the tapes, and to further assure absolute confidentiality, the interviewees will be guaranteed that neither their names nor that of their company will be released. Hence, while the cases will be reported in all necessary detail, the description of the actual firms will be confined to general geographic and industry characteristics.

A last provision that must be mentioned is that in these cases where either the researcher and/or the interview participant is unable to conduct the interview in their native tongue, a fellow researcher from the country in question, is asked to join in at the actual interviews, to provide the greatest comfort to the interviewee, if the need should arise to speak in their native tongue.[263]

The cases at stake are Denmark and Sweden, where all interviews will be conducted in English. In the cases of Austria, Germany and Switzerland all interviews will be conducted in German.

3.1.2 The cases

The number of countries involved in the study was previously mentioned to be five. In the countries of Austria, Denmark, Sweden and Switzerland one

---

[261] Mugler, 1995

[262] Strauss & Corbin, 1990

[263] the author would like to express his gratitude to colleagues at the Copenhagen Business School, Denmark and Jönköping International Business School, Sweden respectively for agreeing to be co-interviewers and providers of language assistance; their time and assistance was greatly appreciated.

case was recruited, while in Germany three cases were obtained. This brings the total number of actual cases to seven.

The number of interviews within a case diverges as well. From a theoretical perspective the attainment of single case interviews suffices. However, if additional interviews were offered by the firm, the offer was accepted as this gave the researcher a chance to further familiarize himself with the environment, and also receive additional information from a non-entrepreneur perspective. Single case interviews were conducted in Denmark, Germany (in two of the three cases), and Switzerland. In the Austrian case and the remaining German case, one additional interview was conducted. It should be noted though that these interviews sometimes started with a single person, then another person joined, and after a while one of the people left again, etc. The point of detailing is to show that for accountability interviews were broken down to the individual, although an interview might have been a group interview becoming a single interview, or vice versa.

In the Swedish case a total of four interviews were conducted and taped. This brings the total number of interviews to 12. All interviews were scheduled for approximately one hour, however the average interview was more in the range of 90 minutes.

The ensuing table aggregates the descriptive data for a better overview.

Country:	# of cases:	# of interviews:
Austria	1	2
Denmark	1	1
Germany	3	4
Sweden	1	4
Switzerland	1	1
Total:	7	12

Table 2: Case statistics

The actual cases and their results are portrayed in the results section[264].

---

[264] cf. section 4.1 on page 89

3.2 Basic grounded theory procedures[265]

Although grounded theory is a methodological innovation, discussed at length in previous sections[266], it does subscribe to some rigor of method. In the following section, basic empirical premises are stated and a brief overview of data coding procedures is presented.

3.2.1 Theoretical sensitivity

Theoretical sensitivity is a quality inherent to varying degrees in every researcher, which essentially enables the researcher to recognize what is important in data and give it meaning. Some practical suggestions to increase theoretical sensitivity are: a) to periodically step back and reflect, b) to maintain an attitude of scepticism, and c) to follow the research procedures provided.

3.2.2 The use of literature

Traditionally, grounded theory has stood out from other research methodologies in that its researchers tried to maintain a mind free of pre-conceived notions. One way to assure that was to postpone a literature review until the empirical research had been carried out.

In its extreme, however, that demand cannot be maintained, since it would be unusually difficult to perform the task of erasing all memory and all knowledge on demand. But that understanding certainly cannot be the assumed purpose of the grounded theory methodology. Rather, the methodology suggests engaging in the reading of technical and non-technical literature and then periodically checking it against the knowledge and insights gained from the data. But most of all, the methodology advises against becoming captive of any of the literature read since doing so would be adopting pre-conceived notions.

---

[265] the entailing section is largely based on Strauss & Corbin, 1990
[266] cf. section 2.2 on page 29

3.2.3 Coding procedures in grounded theory

In grounded theory there are three major types of coding, which are to be applied to recorded and transcribed textual data: a) open coding, b) axial coding, and c) selective coding.

3.2.3.1 Open coding

Open coding is the analytic process by which concepts are identified and developed in terms of their properties and dimensions.

3.2.3.2 Axial coding

Axial coding involves a complex process of inductive and deductive thinking in which comparisons are made and sub-categories are discovered and then linked to the paradigm model. This means that the categories discovered through open coding are focused and sub-ordinated and/or re-linked, which is accomplished by developing causal conditions, but also involves context, strategies of action and/or interaction and consequences.

3.2.3.3 Selective coding

Selective coding entails selecting the core category, systematically relating it to other categories, validating those relationships, and filling in categories that need further refinement.

Also of vital importance is the *constant comparative* method, through which development of a systematic theory is assured. In the constant comparative method, one compares the incidents applicable to each category; in other words, comparing incidents prevents same or similar phenomena from being given a different name.

Another important element in research is *validation*. In grounded theory, there are two complimenting steps to validation: a) literature may help to validate emerging theoretical concepts, and b) relationships are validated against data during all steps of the theory building. The greatest emphasis is placed on validation of the theory through the data.

The grounded theory procedure must be continued until the point of theoretical saturation is reached, that is, that point in time when no new categories emerge from the data, the category development is dense, and the theoretical relationships are well established and validated.

3.3 The secondary data

The preceding part of this chapter was concerned mainly with the nature of the qualitative data collected in five European countries and the procedures for its collection and analysis. In chapter four, "Results", this primary data will be used to develop a core process model for family business.

In the following part of this methodology chapter, a secondary, quantitative data set will be introduced in an attempt to partially validate that process model which will have been derived from the primary, qualitative data. Phrased in methodological terms, the quantitative, secondary data is utilized to provide triangulated confirmation of the findings from the qualitative data.

This secondary data was collected annually between 1990 and 1995 in eight European countries. As will become clear in chapter four through a detailed description of this secondary data, the attempt to validate that process model will not be entirely successful. That success will have been limited for two reasons. First the questionnaire used to gather the secondary data was not designed for, or based on, the proposed model. Second, the number of data points in the secondary data does not satisfy the methodological requirements of a robust longitudinal process model. Nevertheless, partial success at validation is possible if some indications of movement and direction can be demonstrated.

In this section, the secondary data will be introduced in four steps. The first will be an overview of the INTERSTRATOS project - its goals, strategies and institutions involved in it. The next step will be a brief description of the questionnaire and its design. The third step then will be a brief overview of the collected data. Finally, the fourth step will be a presentation of the statistical techniques and encircling issues.

3.3.1 The INTERSTRATOS project[267]

The INTERSTRATOS research group was formed in 1990 in succession of a previous STRATOS research group and consists of institutional members from the following eight countries[268]: Austria, Belgium, Finland, Great Britain, The Netherlands, Norway, Sweden and Switzerland. The purpose of this longitudinal research program was to explore the strategies used by small and medium-sized manufacturing enterprises in coping with changes in their respective task environments. Firms were differentiated according to whether they were operating only in domestic markets, were operating as exporters, or were operating as international businesses. Five industries were selected from which to collect information and data; they were the food, furniture, electronics, mechanical engineering and the textiles industry.

A uniform questionnaire was designed and translated into the languages of the participating countries. The research objectives of INTERSTRATOS can be stated as follows:

1. How do changes in competitive conditions influence product strategy, export orientation, and degree of cooperation in small and medium sized firms?
2. What patterns of internationalization behavior can be observed?
3. Do changes in the values of entrepreneurs correlate with changes in the task environment?

---

[267] the author gratefully acknowledges the Swiss Research Institute of Small Business and Entrepreneurship at the University of St. Gallen, and in particular its Director Prof. Dr. Pleitner, for making available the data and information materials pertaining to the INTERSTRATOS study and permitting their use in this study; a further grateful acknowledgment is also extended to Ms. Margrit Habersaat, who made sure all relevant INTERSTRATOS materials (data, questionnaire, code book) were readily available and accessible
[268] there is data for an additional country: France; however their participation was limited to 1992

A complete overview of the study design and pertinent questions is presented in the first INTERSTRATOS report[269].

3.3.2 *The questionnaire*[270]

The German version of the questionnaire is four pages long. The variables in the model can be classified and categorized as:

1. the exogenous variables
   - entrepreneur/manager characteristics
   - entrepreneur/manager values and attitudes
   - firm and structure
   - contextual constraints/ task environment
2. the endogenous independent variables
   - corporate strategy (product, market and geographic scope)
   - business strategy (export orientation and degree of cooperation)
3. the endogenous dependent variables
   - business performance (domestic and export sales)

The main measures used in the study are: 1. nationality, 2. region, 3. degree of ownership, 4. entrepreneur/manager values, 5. entrepreneur/manager work experience, 6. use of information sources, 7. industry, 8. size of firm, 9. type of production, 10. form of order servicing, 11. changes in competitive conditions, 12. changes in factor markets, 13. changes in constraints and inducements for international operations, 14. product scope, 15. market scope, 16. geographic scope, 17. key success factors, 18. import strategy, 19. form of export orientation, 20. degree of cooperation, 21. total net sales, 22. domestic sales, and 23. export sales.

For measurement operationalizations and item scales, consult the INTERSTRATOS report[271].

---

[269] Haahti, 1993

[270] a German version of the questionnaire is available from the Swiss Research Institute of Small Business and Entrepreneurship at the University of St. Gallen

[271] Haahti, 1993

80

3.3.3 The data

As the data collection was begun in 1990, a first data set of that year was compiled in 1991. Similarly the procedure was carried out until 1995. Hence, a total of five data sets exist. The simple descriptive statistics for these five data sets are given in Table 3.

Data set label:	Year collected:	Reference year:	Sample size:	Number of variables:	Percentage of Family Businesses:
IS91	1991	1990	5091	331	71.1%
IS92	1992	1991	5777	341	71.2%
IS93	1993	1992	4394	357	70.3%
IS94	1994	1993	3903	342	64%
IS95	1995	1994	3571	332	70.8%

Table 3: Data set descriptive statistics

Also, it must be noted that in the context of the INTERSTRATOS study a family business was defined as such if *one family retained over 50 percent of equity*. This definition is essentially congruent with the more abstract definition introduced earlier in this research[272].

3.3.4 Statistical techniques

The structure of the data sets will permit categorizing firms as family firms versus non-family firms. The purpose in utilizing this data set will be to partially validate the to be presented family business model, which will be grounded in data taken solely from family businesses. This secondary data will allow for the attempt to validate, while controlling for the family business variable.

Hence, the analysis must attempt to segregate and determine the effect of family firms versus non-family firms. The statistical techniques available for this kind of analysis are the discriminant and logit or probit regression models. Since the dependent variable here is dichotomous, logit or probit

---

[272] cf. section 2.1.1 on page 13

models are generally preferred over discriminant analysis for doing classification regression. One reason for this preference is that the assumption of multivariate-normal distribution characteristics in discriminant analysis is not reasonable[273]. The logit[274] and probit models are then estimated by means of the maximum likelihood technique[275].

Even though most econometricians recommend a logit model for modeling with a dichotomous dependent variable[276], alternative modeling with probit is attempted. Trying to use another model seems not so far fetched, especially when the rather similar distribution functions of the logit and probit model is taken into account. The probit model includes all explanatory variables specified for the logit model.

3.3.5 Testing for assumption violations

When employing regression techniques, special care must be taken not to violate any regression assumptions. Hence, the following tests will be employed to detect possible multi-collinearity between the independent variables, and to assess homoskedasticity. Since logit and probit models are particularly sensitive to misspecifications[277], special attention is paid to the occurrence of heteroskedasticity, i.e., the violation of homoskedasticity.

3.3.5.1 Heteroskedasticity

Econometric modeling makes the assumption of constant error variance (homoskedasticity). When this assumption is violated and unequal variance exists, heteroskedasticity prevails. With heteroskedasticity present, the ordinary least-squares estimation places more weight on observations with large error variances. Hence, a very good fit of the regression line can be observed in the large-variance portion of the data. Thus, the estimators are still unbiased and consistent, but not efficient.[278]

---

[273] cf. Kennedy, 1993:236

[274] cf. Pindyck & Rubinfeld, 1991:258

[275] cf. Kennedy, 1993:230

[276] cf. chapter 10 of Pindyck & Rubinfeld, 1991

[277] cf. Menard, 1995:58-65

[278] Pindyck & Rubinfeld, 1991:127-128

In order to determine heteroskedasticity any one of the following three tests can be administered: Goldfeld-Quandt test, Breusch-Pagan test, or White test[279]. A number of corrective measures for heteroskedasticity also exist. Further information about these is provided by Pindyck & Rubinfeld.[280]

However, in special cases such as data grouping, statistical theory suggests the existence of heteroskedasticity by the very nature of the data[281]. Within these five data sets, the dependent variable not only consists of grouped data, but is also of a dichotomous nature (family business: yes or no), which leads one to expect the detection of heteroskedasticity by virtue of the theory.

With the aforementioned data set, two tests for heteroskedasticity will be used in SAS to prove the existence of heteroskedasticity. In order to execute these tests a regular (ordinary-least-squares) regression model has to be programmed and administered.

The first test provides the "consistent covariance of estimates" table, while the second test examines the "first and second moment specification". The covariance matrix indicates heteroskedasticity by any of the estimates having high absolute values. The test of the first and second moment specification, which assesses the fit of the specification model, confirms the existence of heteroskedasticity, which is evident in the large chi-square value. As expected because of theory, all five data sets display significant heteroskedasticity.

3.3.5.2 Multi-Collinearity

Another assumption in the multiple regression model is that there is no exact linear relationship between the independent variables in the model. Multicollinearity arises when two or more variables are highly, but not perfectly, correlated with each other. In the case of existing multicollinearity, very high standard errors for the regression parameter will

---

[279] cf. Pindyck & Rubinfeld, 1991:132-136
[280] cf. Pindyck & Rubinfeld, 1991:129-132
[281] cf. Kennedy, 1993:125

surface.[282] SAS permits testing for multicollinearity through collinearity diagnostics, such as the variance inflation factor. The utilization and application of these tests, as well as possible corrective measures, is detailed later[283].

3.3.6 Statistical procedures

The above mentioned logit and probit models are invoked in the SAS program with their respective commands of 'proc logistics' and 'proc probit'. The data will be analyzed in chronological order. The results of the modeling efforts are presented in the tables in sections 4.4.4.1 - 4.4.4.5, beginning on page 108.

The first regression test will use all variables in the model and give an order score, indicating the contributing value of each individual variable.

The second test will perform a stepwise regression, including only those variables which retain individual explanatory power above the 0.05 level of significance.

A third test will provide the summary output and test statistics for the logistic regression along with a classification table providing more specific prediction results for various probability levels. Additional test statistics for multicollinearity and heteroskedasticity will be included, utilizing an ordinary-least-squares regression.

In the cases where multicollinearity will be detected, an additional regression will be performed, dropping the variable(s) which are assumed to be the cause of multicollinearity. This way multicollinearity can usually be eliminated[284]. Unless further specified, no further corrective measures will be taken since the problem is usually assumed to be of minor importance to, and have little effect upon, the overall model, or to have been diminished merely by dropping the variable.

An additional logit regression will also be performed, excluding the variable(s) detected to cause multicollinearity. This logit regression result can then be compared to the initial logit results.

---

[282] cf. Pindyck & Rubinfeld, 1991:83-84

[283] cf. section 4.4.4 on page 105

[284] cf. Kennedy, 1993

Lastly, a probit regression will be performed to test a) whether indeed logit was the better instrument for this model, and b) whether the results of the logit and probit model are generally of the same magnitude, which would exclude possible gross mis-specifications of the model.

The interpretation of the results will be detailed in chapter 5.

Next is the detailing of the implications of using grounded theory and organizational ecology conjectures in developing an evolutionary family business ecology.

3.4 The utilization of grounded theory and ecological conjectures for family business considerations

Basic grounded theory allows and encourages the researcher to examine a study setting without any specific pre-conceived notions; hence the name grounded theory, that is, theory grounded and deeply rooted in the actual data. Additionally, a researcher may choose to integrate certain existing theoretical conjectures in the grounding of a new theory[285]. In this way, existing theory or parts of it may be further developed. As was explained earlier in this study, the field of family business has practically no overarching general theory and this research attempts to fill that void. However, certain theoretical conjectures from other research streams may be incorporated and applied as a basis from which to develop a new holistic family business theory.

The basic assumption found in ecological and other evolution process theories of selection, variation, competition and retention is retained for this study. Although recent ecological theory has argued that adaptation of both the organizations' core elements and periphery elements is possible[286] - though at the cost of re-setting the firm's "life clock" - this study contends that, theoretically speaking, only peripheral adaptation is possible. The basis for this contention was laid out earlier when Lakatos' research methodology was analyzed and his epistemological beliefs were adopted.[287]

---

[285] cf. Glaser & Strauss, 1967; Strauss & Corbin, 1990
[286] cf. Amburgey et al., 1993; Havemann, 1992
[287] cf. section 2.2.4 on page 41

Nevertheless, this study argues that, on empirical grounds, the phenomenon of family business longevity suggests - and offers some proof - that additional processes, distinct from the above mentioned four (selection, variation, competition and retention), are at work, in particular, the initial processes of imprinting. This unknown and unexplored process, it is proposed, entails an imprinting of core values and attributes on the firm which guide it throughout its life and various business cycles. The current literature also assumes a very aware and pro-active firm. For example, Burgelman in his attempt to bridge ecological models with strategic choice, asserts that intra-organizational selection of competing strategies occurs. Then, once a strategy is actively selected within the organization, it would enable the firm to adapt at the organizational level.[288] This model, however, does not account for how and by what means those firms are guided that do not have an explicit strategy, let alone an intra-organizational strategy competition.

Phenomenologically, part of the answer could be inherent in the lack of a language common to the research community and the firms. Another part of the answer could be different perceptions of the same phenomenon and different means to realize them, for example, strategies emanating in action.

Likewise, another conjecture (or part of it), that might be helpful in conceptualizing a family business theory is the assumption in intra-organizational ecology that the opposing forces of selection and adaptation are both at work. Burgelman suggested that selection is at work at the intra-organizational level, while adaptation occurs at the inter-organizational level[289]. Burgelman's suggestion is a step forward from previous ecological research in that it included and bridged selection and adaptation forces[290]; for this reason, his conjecture will be utilized in this research. However, it remains quite unclear why these two forces are still conceived of by ecologists as dichotomous rather than as inter-dependent forces and/or as different aspects on the continuum of evolution forces. This dichotomous

---

[288] Barnett & Burgelman, 1996; Burgelman, 1996; Burgelman & Mittman, 1994

[289] Burgelman, 1996

[290] cf. Tushman & Romanelli, 1990

view of evolution implies that each level of analysis (the intra-organizational, the inter-organizational, the population level, and the community level) is confined to either force (adaptation, selection). On a related note, for a discussion on the debate in ecology research on divergent levels of analysis and its implications, consult Amburgey & Rao[291].

Related to the earlier argument of adaptation of organizational core and periphery elements, the ecology's conjecture regarding the existence of a core is accepted[292]. However, the proposed content will be questioned.

Lastly, as was hinted at above, currently much emphasis in ecological research is placed on the selection-adaptation dichotomy. It was iterated earlier that the outcome of both processes is identical, but still much effort is induced in trying to 'guess' the content of this 'black-box' process, of which only the input and output are known[293]. Early attempts were made by McKelvey to further the knowledge on the issue by pursuing the crux regarding imprinting[294]. It seems that much could be gained by a better understanding on the process of imprinting, since that ultimately will inform researchers in a more detailed way on the input for change processes. Henceforth the conjecture regarding the existence and importance of imprinting is accepted, and to be further utilized and developed.

---

[291] cf. Amburgey & Rao, 1996

[292] Hannan & Freeman, 1989

[293] for a graphical depiction please turn to page 52

[294] cf. McKelvey, 1982

4. RESULTS

Say goodbye to golden yesterdays...
... The best is yet to come.
(Anthony de Mello SJ, 1984[295])

This section on model development represents the heart of this research study and is the first part of the results chapter. It is here that all the previous expositions of methodology, epistemology, literature review, and cases will be brought together to show the emergence of the evolutionary ecology of family business as a distinct organizational form. Stated differently, it is in this section that the 'oscillating' and 'grounding' theory process will surface and become formalized. What was before only theoretical conjecture will now be presented as emerging from within the grounded, empirical data. To be sure, 'emerging' implies by no means though some sort of magical process, rather it is the development of the theory in gradual steps, adhering to the procedure detailed in section 3.2 on page 76, and later validated according to the submitted criteria.

The outline of this chapter is as follows. In the first section (4.1) the family business cases will be described, followed by the core model which was derived from the data (4.2). Next (4.3) are excerpts from the interviews, that is, story-like details which are intended to help show the emergence of core elements, which were formally presented in the prior section. Based on the core model, hypotheses will be developed and the subsequent results from the analysis of the INTERSTRATOS data set will be submitted (4.4).

4.1 Presentation of cases

The procedure for conducting this case research was outlined in the methodology chapter. However, it is only at this juncture that descriptive accounts of the cases will be presented. Following are partial, yet detailed accounts of information particularly relevant to this study. A complete

---

[295] de Mello, 1984:227, 239

picture of the firm is presented, especially in relationship to the proposed core model elements.

At this point, it should be noted that this particular sample displays in some sense a success bias, that is, in the sense that most of these firms have survived beyond the first generation[296]. Although there is nothing inherently wrong with this kind of bias, an awareness of the fact is essential. Besides that definition of success, namely, success via the proxy of generational survival, success through market leadership or through market share is also conceivable.

4.1.1 Austria (case A)

This particular business, which is wholly owned by the family, has been in existence for about 50 years and is currently under the leadership of the third generation. As a general description, it may be said that the company is involved in the international transportation business.

The sole pursuit of the company is in the aforementioned international industry, while varying emphasis is placed on the different geographic markets served. The level of employment is roughly at the high end of the medium size definition (200-249 employees). The third generation, the one currently in charge, is college educated, and the succession from the second to this third generation was planned.

4.1.2 Denmark (case D)

The Danish business studied is also fully owned by the family. This business has been in existence for approximately 60 years and has involved three generations. Currently, the second generation is still at the helm of the company and the third generation is fully involved, although with no concrete succession plans. The company is engaged in the general manufacturing industry and specializes in two basic branches, industrial manufacturing and the production of luxury products. Employment is at the lower end of the medium size spectrum (50-99 employees). By choice, the company is involved in both domestic and foreign markets.

---

[296] cf. page 17 for generational survival statistics

4.1.3 Germany

4.1.3.1 Case G1

The first German case is a family firm that was founded some 120 years ago. It is currently run by a member of the fourth generation. The company focuses on two basic products, both of which are within the realm of international machine manufacturing. Ownership of the company is dispersed widely throughout the rather large family. The issue of succession has not yet been dealt with. The possibility of a successor from within the family is remote. The company's employment level is in the 200 to 249 employee class.

4.1.3.2 Case G2

The second German firm is wholly owned by the family and currently under the management of the second generation. Founded approximately 50 years ago, this manufacturing firm has two basic product lines, both of which by their nature involve the firm in international markets. The firm is recognized as the market leader in Europe in the category of its main product line. The employment level is between 100 and 149 employees.

4.1.3.3 Case G3

The third German family business is still under the direction of its founder, who became an entrepreneur over 30 years ago. Today, in addition to the main firm, several other businesses have been founded and have become part of the overall structure. The second generation of the family is involved in the business, but the founder retains ownership and control. The focus of this venture is mainly on personal and capital financial investments. The firm is in the employment category of 100 to 149 employees. Because of the nature of the industry, the firm's business is mostly localized and consequently confined within the borders of Germany. No active succession planning has been put in place. The firm is one of the two or three biggest in its industry in Germany.

Although this firm has relatively low numbers of employees (in contrast to other firms mentioned before), it has an annual turnover which is about ten times greater than that of an aforementioned manufacturing company, while maintaining equal employment figures. This fact helps illuminate the complexity of dimensions across industries inasmuch as both firms are leaders in their respective market, namely, Germany and Europe, but with a varying number of input requirements.

4.1.4 Sweden (case S1)

The Swedish company examined in this case was founded almost 35 years ago and is currently in the hands of the second generation. This company focuses on two lines of specialty manufacturing, which account for almost equal parts of its output and conducts its business in the international marketplace. This firm belongs to the employment class of 150 to 199 employees. Since the current chief executive is still many years away from retirement, the firm has no active plans for succession.

4.1.5 Switzerland (case S2)

The Swiss company involved in the study has been in business for roughly 70 years. The current executive and owner belongs to the third generation. This company diversified into the manufacturing of specialties and luxury goods, each of which account for approximately half of the sales. Its employment level falls in the 50 to 99 employee category.

It should be noted at this point that none of the entrepreneurs interviewed suggested that they had taken any particular steps in light of the European Union. Most conceived of it as a gradual process that up to now inflicted more hassles than benefits upon their businesses. Their statements suggest that the European Union was thought of neither as a great opportunity nor as a threat.

The following Table 4 is provided for a graphic overview of the basic demographic information.

92

Country:	Case:	Generation:	Employment level:	Product lines:
Austria	A	3rd	200-249	1
Denmark	D	2nd/3rd	50-99	2
Germany	G1	4th	200-249	2
Germany	G2	2nd	100-149	2
Germany	G3	1st	100-149	2
Sweden	S1	2nd	150-199	2
Switzerland	S2	3rd	50-99	2

Table 4: Case Demographics

4.2 The model

The evolutionary ecology theory of family business may be introduced in simple steps by positing that family businesses have a different form, in contrast to other organizational forms. Specifically, it is assumed that they have a distinguishable *family business **core*** and a *periphery*. This proposition of the division of core and periphery is in concordance with Lakatos' supposition[297].

The following is a description of the organizational hard core and a logical argumentation for this hard core; however, a more exact detailing of the concept emergence will be given in the following individual sections, which permit elaborations on the emergence of these conjectures in the actual data.

If one accepts Lakatos' model of hard core vs. periphery, it can be logically inferred that the task at hand is the demonstration of the (rarely mutable) hard core elements, since the periphery's components are subsequently manifold and change over time. Figure 6 depicts the environment in which an organization is set. This organization consists of the two basic elements, the core and the periphery. The organizational boundaries of the form are determined by the environmental infrastructure. The center of the organization is the core. The core retains a number of elements which rarely ever change. Also, the core's strength is a function of its impenetrably hard outer covering.

---

[297] cf. Lakatos, 1970; Lakatos, 1978; Lakatos & Musgrave, 1970

On the other hand the periphery's elements surround the core but are bound to the organizational form by its outer boundaries. The periphery's elements are loosely connected, and hence rarely ever maintain a consistent and lasting constellation, quite in contrast to the hard core. And while the core is protected by a hard shell, the outer boundaries represent a threshold, but not one which is impassable. That is to say, many elements and ideas arise in the larger environment, some of which are more proximate, while others are more distant within and/or from the organization in question.

With the passing of time the distance of these various objects to one another may change, and so does the environmental infrastructure and conditions. When these changes occur, some formerly outer elements are now able to become part of the organization in question, while formerly inner elements are no longer able to maintain their right to exist within the organizational boundaries, and change to an outer position. However, none of these elements or ideas are able to penetrate the hard core in the course of this evolution, rather forces of greater magnitude would be necessary to transform the hard core. An example of such a force would be some sort of revolution, which may come in many different forms – revolutionary new ways of thought and logic, revolutionary metamorphosis of infrastructure, or revolutionary innovations in technology[298], to name just a few of those that are conceivable.

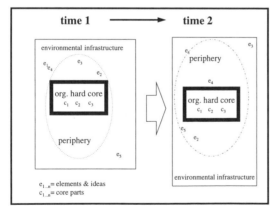

Figure 6: Family business core, periphery and environment

[298] cf. Anderson & Tushman, 1990; Tushman & Anderson, 1986; Tushman & Romanelli, 1990 for exemplars of conceptual and explanatory research outlining the details of a radical technological change process

The hard core of the family business retains characteristics which enable the development of a certain process model. These core characteristics are:

1. simplicity;
2. focus on core business;
3. absolute belief in, dedication to, and enthusiasm for the business;
4. distinctive values and principles; and
5. system-based motivators like incentives and rewards.

Before elaborating on these five broad categories, it should be noted that all of these categories will be shown in the latter section to have been derived from actual data, and consequently are presented here in more general yet abstract fashion, allowing accessible exposition, and by no means too abstract non-falsifiable classification. A graphical depiction of the family business hard core is provided in Figure 7.

In the ensuing subsection the individual cases will be presented. The delineation of each core aspect, however will be discussed in chapter five.

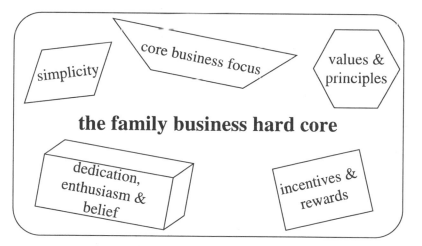

Figure 7: Family business core elements

4.3 The core elements as found embedded in the case data

In the previous section the general model for understanding family firms was explained, and the individual family businesses were presented as particular cases. As mentioned earlier, the core elements emerged and were developed as the main categories from within the collected data. In this section, now, the observation of different parts of these core elements will be recapitulated in the context of their environment, and certain story-like aspects of these core elements will be presented. These aspects will then help to illustrate the *refined* model to be presented in the next chapter; this model will show the core elements in their *process* relation to one another.

One organization, in telling its story, stated that they had no strategy or stated financial goal and declared that their sole purpose was to help people (by the means of their business) and that their concrete actions flowed simply from that purpose. The firm's innovation capacity resulted from their ability to integrate their product offerings with service, a practice previously unheard of in this industry. Again, this points out that they valued being in business as a means of helping people. The organization's guiding principle – personified in the actions of the entrepreneur – was their belief in honesty and hard work. To be sure, no business can survive without profitability, but that was not a motivator for this organization's being in business. Also, when this firm responds that they have no strategy, they mean that they have nothing that resembles what the academicians or consultants describe as strategy, whether they use the specific term *strategy* or not. For the observer, however, the presence and paramount importance of an unarticulated strategy became clear, not only through the obvious market dominance of the firm, but also through the verbal expression which comprised much of a strategy except the word.
Regarding rewards, the organization adhered to a strongly articulated policy of fairness, i.e., fair employee relations and adequate, fair wages.

Another organization emphasized the need to build and maintain a business based on trust – trust, both in the organization and in its employees and customers. Its ability to simplify the complex became clear when it was stated that the need to internationalize was "painstakingly clear", that is, there was no choice or other option, at least as far as the entrepreneur was concerned. A similar view prevailed in the matter of succession. When the older generation was increasingly plagued by health problems, succession "just had to happen". A guiding principle of this organization was a deep belief in itself and its abilities. Organizational self esteem – not arrogance –

was an explicit cornerstone of the organization. This firm also stated that its current size (in number of employees) was quite intentional; growth was not even contemplated. Of intrinsic value to the organization was an absolute identification with the firm and its products.

The next organization placed high value on its customers, which was clear from its focus on customer satisfaction, its maintenance of two-way communication channels, and its desire to "live close to the customer". Its overriding principle was that all employees must have some affiliation with, and affinity to, that particular family firm's background if they are to be sensitive to the firm's concerns and products. A concrete example would be that of a family business auto manufacturer who hired only employees coming from affiliated backgrounds, such as people whose parents were car mechanics. Such a stringent requirement is better understood in the context of their vision statement, which emphasizes that the firm is their whole purpose in life, their vocation. For this firm innovation meant a planned evolution in step with the customer, of course. The entrepreneur said his guiding principles were humility and honesty coupled with aggressiveness in the market. He later articulated this remarkable morale and belief: it is not the big firms eating the small ones, but rather the quick firms eating the slow ones. This entrepreneur's simple insight was that the firm must grow, however gradually, to assure survival. The family business and its culture were considered their own motivation inasmuch as it represented stability as well as a holistic way of life. Another motivation expressed was the desire to create further employment.

The next firm established as its core value the belief that good lived out behavior of the leadership, and only that, motivates imitation of the same and more. An externally-directed core principle was the necessity to keep close to the customers. Innovation was seen as a self-propelling process, facilitated through the company's keeping an 'ear to the market'.

The next company talked of the evolution of its core business, meaning that market demands and general technological advancements clearly showed that the business which exists today is different from the business in its founding phase. The important issue is the ability to stay with a single business idea despite its evolution, and also to show that a core business must not mean a static focus. However, it was also stressed that focus clearly meant the establishment of a business presence in a niche market. The rewards the company was able to articulate were stability and guaranteed long-time employment. Similarly, internal motivation was attributed to the care for the family's well being. In their own sense-making this firm stated that any kind of long-term strategy was ridiculous and stupid, while on the other hand they also expressed that, in order to retain market leadership, the firm must maintain a 'finger on the market pulse'. An additional reward the entrepreneur identified was the company's team decision-making policy. Lastly, emphasis was placed on the existence of institutional (mutual) commitment, and its stability.

The next firm in sequence argued that money was a manifested non-value and non-motivator. Of high value to the firm were continuity and stability. The articulated core value was the firm's ability to be a leader through continuous innovation. Hence progressiveness was presented as another guiding principle.

The last firm involved in this research also placed a high value on stability. Belonging to the family of the business was seen as a reward. Strategy was again not an active part of their vocabulary, yet it emerged in actions. Also innovation was not a formalized process, but rather an emanation and maturation of co-incidentally incurring ideas.

The purpose of detailing the 'stories' of these firms was to point out the proposed core elements embedded in the actual data. It was decided to present these aspects within their full context rather than as excerpts from the cases grouped according to the core categories. The latter approach would have detracted too much from the richness of these individual stories, and this richness was vital to the process of deriving these core parts. By retaining these stories in their totality, it was hoped that the reader would experience and see more clearly the process whereby the core categories are derived and emerge.

In the following section the INTERSTRATOS data set described earlier[299] will be utilized to examine the proposed model of the family business core; this will permit a degree of generalizability.

4.4 The Statistical Analysis of the INTERSTRATOS data

Because the INTERSTRATOS data set is being used here for the purpose of validating a grounded theory model, it is necessary to formulate the research questions in hypothetical form and to indicate the relevant proxy variables. The grounded theory model which was submitted earlier in this chapter, serves as the basis for the research questions.

To briefly recapitulate the main thrust of the model. The proposed model, developed from grounded theory distinguishes between the core and periphery of an organization. The assumption is that the peripheral elements are those which are weakly linked to the organizational core in that they may change position in relation to the core over time. This means, for example, that an element such as marketing strategy may vary over time in its importance and function vis-à-vis an organization's core. The core elements are those whose relative importance and mutual relationships in an organization do not vary over time, suggesting a spatial fixation and retention of the strength of relationship ties. The process by which the core elements are determined and differentiated from non-core elements is explained as a kind of initial imprinting process.[300]

Since the distinction between the organizational core and periphery was made, this research has proposed the following elements as the model's core components. These core elements, specific to family businesses are:
1. simplicity;
2. focus on core business;
3. absolute belief in, dedication to, and enthusiasm for the business;
4. distinctive values and principles;
5. system-based motivators like incentives and rewards.

---

[299] cf. section 3.3 on page 78 ff.

[300] for a graphical depiction of this model please turn to page 94 (Figure 6)

4.4.1 The hypotheses

Based on these empirically derived core elements, the research questions can now be proposed as hypotheses, while the following section (4.4.2) will discuss the proxy construction.

Propositions regarding the whole of the core and the distinguishability of family businesses.

> H1: The organizational core of family businesses is likely to be significantly different as compared to non-family businesses.
>
> > *(distinctiveness of whole family business core)*

> H2: The organizational core of family businesses is likely to remain constant over time.
>
> > *(distinctiveness of whole family business core over time)*

Propositions regarding the significance of individual core elements of family businesses.

> H3: Placing high value on the importance of the quality of management is likely to be an element of the family business core.
>
> > *(individual proxy for values and principles)*

> H4: Placing high value on the importance of the reputation of the firm is likely to be an element of the family business core.
>
> > *(individual proxy for values and principles)*

> H5: Placing high value on the importance of the quality of employees is likely to be an element of the family business core.
>
> > *(individual proxy for values and principles)*

> H6: Placing high value on the importance of the quality of continuing education of management is likely to be an element of the family business core.
>
> > *(individual proxy for system motivators)*

100

H7: Placing high value on the importance of the quality of continuing education of employees is likely to be an element of the family business core.

(individual proxy for system motivators)

H8: The family business entrepreneur is likely to have a significantly higher number of years of business experience than a non-family business entrepreneur.

(individual proxy for dedication to business)

H9: Placing high value on the avoidance of change is likely to be an element of the family business core.

(individual proxy for core business focus, and simplicity)

H10: Placing high value on the belief that the family firm should remain in family hands is likely to be an element of the family business core.

(individual proxy for system incentives and rewards, and simplicity)

H11: Placing high value on the importance of behavior according to ethical principles is likely to be an element of the family business core.

(individual proxy for distinctive values, simplicity)

H12: Placing high value on the prioritizing of business affairs over family life is likely to be an element of the family business core.

(individual proxy for distinctive values)

H13: Placing high value on the importance of product quality is likely to be an element of the family business core.

(individual proxy for core business focus, and simplicity)

4.4.2 Variables and proxy constructs

In the previous section the hypotheses were presented and a parenthetical indication of their intended proxy was provided. Now, in order to discuss the proxy construction in relation to the hypotheses, an exact knowledge of the included variables and their respective scales is warranted.

Within these data sets the following variables were included for the analysis; the first variable (FAMBUS) is the dependent variable.

Variable label:	Variable description:	Scale:
FAMBUS	Family Business	Yes/No
MGT_QUAL	Importance of quality of management	1-5 (Likert)
REPUT	Importance of reputation of firm	1-5 (Likert)
EMP_QUAL	Importance of quality of employees	1-5 (Likert)
PROD_QUL	Importance of product quality	1-5 (Likert)
CONTED_M	Importance of continuing education of the entrepreneur	1-5 (Likert)
CONTED_E	Importance of continuing education of the employees	1-5 (Likert)
EXPER	Years of experience	continuous numeric
CHG_AVER	Change should be avoided	1-5 (Likert)
FB_CONT	Firm should remain in family hands	1-5 (Likert)
ETH_BEH	Importance of behavior according to ethical principles	1-5 (Likert)
BUSVSFAM	Business has priority over family life	1-5 (Likert)

Table 5: Data Set Variables Label, Name and Scale

4.4.2.1 Hypotheses concerning the individual core elements

Hypotheses 3 through 5 are intended to validate the core element of values and principles. It is suggested that valuing the quality of management and a firm's employees, along with a genuine concern for a firm's reputation is a direct, though incomplete, proxy for certain values and principles. Though an incomplete measurement, the existence of three proxies provides some comfort in the reliability of the measurement.

Hypotheses 6 and 7 are suggested to validate the core element of system-based motivators like incentives and rewards. Here it is argued that, in a system that does not care about motivation or provision of incentives and rewards, little or no value would be placed on continuing education. Continuing education is assumed to be mutually beneficial to the employee and the employer; this suggests that continuing education is an important mutual incentive.

Hypothesis 8 is assumed to be a single-item validation of the core element called belief in, dedication to and enthusiasm for the business. This assumption is that, without the existence of this core element, the number of years at the family company would be significantly fewer. Without greater belief in the firm (than the non-family-business entrepreneur) the entrepreneur's dedication to the firm would not be distinguishable as measured in years of affiliation with the company. However, since this is not the only possible interpretation of this variable, in addition to this being a single item validation attempt, the proxy can at best be called weak.

Hypothesis 9 is an attempt to validate the core categories of core business focus and simplicity. The explanation is that an avoidance of change would indicate a strong focus on the core business and an ability to simplify, meaning an ability to make sense and distinguish between radical and incremental change. However, the construction of this variable is admittedly rather ambiguous and must be treated with great caution and as a rather weak proxy.

Hypothesis 10 is suggested to validate the two core elements of incentives and rewards, and of simplicity. The assumption is made that the reason for the entrepreneur wanting to keep the firm in family hands is (a) to provide one of the rewards planned for the successors and (b) to maintain the firm as an overarching, yet simplifying system. Once again, however, this explanation cannot claim to be the only possible interpretation.

Hypotheses 11 and 12 are attempts to validate the single core category of values and principles; additionally, these two hypotheses serve as a secondary validation of the core element called simplicity. It is assumed that the ability to value ethical behavior and to prioritize (and keep apart) affairs, is an indicative validation of the existence of distinctive values and principles. Additionally, it is argued that such behavior further indicates the ability to simplify in light of the existing multiplicity of other options and modes of conduct. These are weak proxies in so far as the above interpretation is only one of many because of the rather general phrasing of the survey question.

Hypothesis 13 assumes to be validating the core categories of focus on core business and of simplicity. The argument is made that valuing high product quality is opposite of valuing diversification, and that those who cannot distinguish themselves will branch out in more products. However, the ambiguous phrasing of the question leaves much to be desired, in terms of reliably measuring only these two core categories.

Despite the fact that most of the variables introduced are rather weak proxies for validating the core elements, in most every category – except for belief in, dedication to, and enthusiasm for the firm – multiple measurements were nevertheless constructed to increase the overall reliability.

4.4.2.2 Hypotheses concerning the whole core model

Hypothesis 1 aims at determining whether or not the combination of the above-outlined proxies for the individual core elements constitutes the family business core, which is distinguishable from non-family businesses. Hypothesis 2 takes for granted that the holistic family business core is indeed determinable; however, it questions whether or not that particular core remains distinguishable over time.

4.4.3 Descriptive data set information

Before any statistical analysis could be carried out, it was first necessary to modify the respective data sets to conform to the specifications of this research study, mainly to control for firm size. The chosen size class for this study was that of medium-sized enterprises, defined as firms employing between 50 and 249 people (cf. page 73).

Table 6 below gives the summary statistics for the five data sets utilized.

Data set name:	Number of medium-sized firms:	Number of complete observations:	Number of Family Businesses:
IS91	1173	886	507
IS92	1303	954	534
IS93	964	656	326
IS94	890	688	391
IS95	879	657	360

Table 6: Data Set Summary Statistics

4.4.4 Results and presentation of the statistical analysis

The results of the statistical procedure, which was described in detail in section 3.3.4 on page 81, were transferred into tables to allow for a better overview and better comparability. As the heading indicates, the first column in the following logit tables provides the variable name. The second column provides the normalized coefficients of the first logit regression model with the standard error in parentheses. All significant coefficients are shown in bold type face and their significance level is indicated.

The third column, named Score Chi-Square, provides the results from the stepwise logit regression detailing only those variables that were significant at or above the 0.05 level; also, the absolute magnitude of the numbers indicates their scoring value, that is, the higher the value the more variation they explain and signals the order in which they were entered into the regression.

The fourth column provides the Odds Ratio, which essentially indicates the level of explanatory power each individual variable contributes. For example, a 1.50 value for REPUT (valuing the firms reputation) would mean that the odds of being correctly classified as a family business is multiplied by 50 percent when the judgment about the valuing of a firm's reputation is known.

105

The fifth column entitled the Variance Inflation Factor, is a test for multi-collinearity which was performed during an additional regression analysis. Any variable with a factor above 1.3 (30%) was excluded in the subsequent analysis. A factor of 1.3 would indicate that the existence of multicollinearity accounts for 30 percent of the variance of the variable results. The cut-off point usually is at or above 1.3, when there is an assumption of a need to correct or control for multi-collinearity[301].

Columns six through nine contain the results from the second logit model, which excluded the variables deleted for multi-collinearity.

On the bottom of each table an additional number of test statistics is reported. The first two statistics are the Likelihood Ratio and the Langrange Multiplier (along with the degrees of freedom), which serve as goodness-of-fit tests[302]. Comparability of those statistics to the F-test and R-squared is often inferred, but is not scientifically warranted[303]. The percentage of correctly predicted cases is stated below these statistics.

The last two statistics are the Akaike Information Criterion and the Schwarz Criterion. These values are comparative measures of relative model fit and specification.

In the following probit tables the first column contains the variable name. The second column identifies the coefficient values of the first probit model, which was specified as analogous to the first logit model. All significant values are reported in bold type face and their respective significance levels are indicated. The third and fifth column provide the standard errors of the coefficients.

The second probit model (column four) is also analogous to the second logit model in that the variables assumed to be the cause of multi-collinearity are deleted from the model. At the bottom of the probit tables the Likelihood

---

[301] cf. Kennedy, 1993
[302] cf. Menard, 1995:18-21
[303] cf. Kennedy, 1993:110

Ratio Chi-Square and the Pearson Chi-Square (along with their respective degrees of freedom) are reported; these statistics are measures of the model's goodness-of-fit. Significance is indicated by bold type face where appropriate. Lastly, the Log-Likelihood which is necessary for computing the likelihood ratio, is reported for the sake of completeness [304].

---

[304] Menard, 1995

4.4.4.1 1991 (IS91)

Variable:	Logit Model 1: coefficient (std. error)	Score Chi-Square	Odds Ratio	Variance Inflation Factor	Logit Model 2: coefficient (std. error)	Score Chi-Square	Odds Ratio	Variance Inflation Factor
Intercept	-1.2379 (.9898)		.	0	-1.3058 (.9708)		.	0
MGT_QUAL	-.0393 (.0093)		.961	1.174	-.0348 (.1184)		.966	1.176
REPUT	.0511 (.0796)		1.052	1.07	.0634 (.0788)		1.065	1.067
EMP_QUAL	-.0823 (.1217)		.921	1.214	-.0725 (.1203)		.930	1.209
PROD_QUL	.0182 (.1390)		1.018	1.067	-.0075 (.1378)		.993	1.066
CONTED_M	-.0318 (.2013)		.969	2.002	-.1204 (.1440)		.887	1.041
CONTED_E	-.1445 (.2013)		.865	1.987	omitted			omitted

Variable:	Logit Model 1: coefficient (std. error)	Score Chi-Square	Odds Ratio	Variance Inflation Factor	Logit Model 2: coefficient (std. error)	Score Chi-Square	Odds Ratio	Variance Inflation Factor
EXPER	.0304* (.0069)	26.38*	1.031	1.093	.0291* (.0068)	24.78*	1.030	1.091
CHG_AVER	.1953" (.1067)	4.39"	1.216	1.153	.1998" (.1061)	4.53"	1.221	1.151
FB_CONT	.3888* (.0747)	45.24*	1.475	1.113	.3968* (.0738)	46.77*	1.487	1.108
ETH_BEH	.0108 (.0848)		1.011	1.031	.0022 (.0830)		1.002	1.028
BUSVSFAM	.0848 (.0725)		1.089	1.043	.0938 (.0714)		1.098	1.041
Likelihood Ratio df	81.79* 11				81.728* 10			
Lagrange Multiplier	76.935*				76.847*			

Variable:	Logit Model 1: coefficient (std. error)	Score Chi-Square	Odds Ratio	Variance Inflation Factor	Logit Model 2: coefficient (std. error)	Score Chi-Square	Odds Ratio	Variance Inflation Factor
Concordant	66.5%				66.3%			
Predicted Cases								
Akaike Information Criterion	1211.7				1235.903			
Schwarz Criterion	1216.487				1240.704			
Note: "p≤.1 ^p≤.01 *p≤.001								

Table 7: Logit Regression Results for INTERSTRATOS 1991

110

In the first logit regression the coefficients for Exper, Chg_aver and Fb_cont are significant. Furthermore, the stepwise regression points to Fb_cont as having the highest overall explanatory effect since its score of 45.24 was found to be the highest. Furthermore, this highest explanatory power is mirrored in its odds ratio of 1.475, meaning that, when the value of Fb_cont is known, the odds of correctly classifying a firm as a family business are multiplied by 47.5 percent.

Because of the existence of multi-collinearity between Conted_m and Conted_e, the latter variable is dropped from the second logit regression. However, this elimination of Conted_e does not change the significance of any coefficients. Fb_cont and Chg_aver remain the most powerful explanatory variables, having a predictive power in the range of 48 percent and 22 percent respectively.

In both logit models the model's overall prediction power is 66 percent, and both indicators of the model's goodness-of-fit test remain highly significant without any drastic change in their respective absolute values.

The Akaike Information Criterion (AIC) and Schwarz Criterion (SC) are, comparatively speaking, slightly better values for the first logit model. So, the first logit model seems to be the better overall explanatory model, given the awareness of the existence of multi-collinearity.

This logit model, therefore, permits the acceptance of the first hypothesis, which concerns the existence of a distinguishable holistic core in family businesses. Also, because of the high significance of the above-mentioned individual variables, hypotheses 8 through 10 can be accepted.

It is important to note that, although no further individual variables were significant, their overall contribution to the model in explanatory power deserves to be acknowledged, and for this reason these variables were retained in the model. Statistically this can be shown by comparing the prediction power of the overall logit model with the prediction power of the stepwise logit regression, which only included individual variables significant above the 0.05 level. The results show that the overall explanation power is lower in the stepwise model, and this justifies the retention of the additional (individually insignificant) variables in the model.

Variable:	Probit Model 1: coefficient	standard error	Probit Model 2: coefficient	standard error
Intercept	-.7333	.608	-.7814	.5968
MGT_QUAL	-.0273	.0732	-.0244	.0727
REPUT	.0296	.0489	.0375	.0485
EMP_QUAL	-.0546	.0746	-.0485	.0737
PROD_QUL	.0126	.0853	-.0029	.0846
CONTED_M	-.0204	.1233	-.0787	.0883
CONTED_E	-.0948	.1233	omitted	
EXPER	.0186*	.0042	.0178*	.0041
CHG_AVER	.1156^	.0632	.1176"	.0628
FB_CONT	.2421*	.0453	.2472*	.0448
ETH_BEH	.0095	.0517	.0043	.0506
BUSVSFAM	.0535	.0444	.0587	.0438
Likelihood Ratio Chi-Square	1127.49*		1151.82*	
df	873		891	
Pearson Chi-Square	880.72		898.57	
Log Likelihood	-563.74		-575.91	
Note: "$p \le .1$ ^ $p \le .01$ * $p \le .001$				

Table 8: Probit Regression Results for INTERSTRATOS 1991

Essentially the probit model confirms the findings of the logit model. The variables Fb_cont, Exper and Chg_aver are significant above the 0.001 and 0.1 level respectively. The goodness-of-fit tests for both probit models are also highly significant, confirming the overall good specification of the model. The probit regression definitely allows acceptance of hypotheses 1 and 8 through 10 for the year 1991.

4.4.4.2 1992 (IS92)

Variable:	Logit Model 1: coefficient (std. error)	Score Chi-Square	Odds Ratio	Variance Inflation Factor	Logit Model 2: coefficient (std. error)	Score Chi-Square	Odds Ratio	Variance Inflation Factor
Intercept	-3.0965 (.8623)		.	0	-3.0402 (.8426)		.	0
MGT_QUAL	.0622 (.1065)		1.064	1.234	.0624 (.1062)		1.064	1.235
REPUT	.1525" (.0789)	5.08"	1.165	1.082	.1648" (.0785)	5.25"	1.179	1.079
EMP_QUAL	.0939 (.1175)		1.098	1.289	.0773 (.1170)		1.080	1.287
PROD_QUL	-.0330 (.1279)		.968	1.181	-.0428 (.1277)		.958	1.182
CONTED_M	-.1193 (.1900)		.888	1.879	-.1075 (.1403)		.898	1.044
CONTED_E	.0164 (.1918)		1.017	1.908	omitted			omitted

Variable:	Logit Model 1: coefficient (std. error)	Score Chi-Square	Odds Ratio	Variance Inflation Factor	Logit Model 2: coefficient (std. error)	Score Chi-Square	Odds Ratio	Variance Inflation Factor
EXPER	.0310* (.0066)	27.87*	1.032	1.061	.0314* (.0065)	28.67*	1.032	1.056
CHG_AVER	.2347" (.0992)	4.79"	1.265	1.126	.2277" (.0987)	5.02"	1.256	1.126
FB_CONT	.4588* (.0731)	64.15*	1.582	1.130	.4763* (.0727)	69.04*	1.610	1.130
ETH_BEH	.0713 (.0846)		1.074	1.021	.0619 (.0838)		1.064	1.019
BUSVSFAM	.0340 (.0700)		1.035	1.049	.0396 (.0691)		1.040	1.044
Likelihood Ratio	108.24*				114.266*			
df	11				10			
Lagrange Multiplier	100.543*				105.798*			

Variable:	Logit Model 1: coefficient (std. error)	Score Chi-Square	Odds Ratio	Variance Inflation Factor	Logit Model 2: coefficient (std. error)	Score Chi-Square	Odds Ratio	Variance Inflation Factor
Concordant Predicted Cases	68.8%				69.2%			
Akaike Information Criterion	1310.87				1329.99			
Schwarz Criterion	1315.73				1334.87			
Note: ^p≤.1 ^p≤.01 *p≤.001								

Table 9: Logit Regression Results for INTERSTRATOS 1992

The results from the logit regression performed on the 1992 data set are even better than the already very good results from the 1991 data. The variables Fb_cont and Exper are reported with coefficients at significance levels above 0.001, while the variables Reput and Chg_aver are significant above the 0.1 level. The stepwise logistic regression even suggests that Reput and Chg_aver are significant above the 0.05 level. The predictive power of Fb_cont is approaching 60 percent with an odds ratio of 58.2 percent, while Chg_aver accounts for an odds ratio of 26.5 percent.

As the 1991 data hinted at principally, there exists categorical multi-collinearity between Conted_e and Conted_m. Therefore, Conted_e was deleted from the second logit regression, and this, as the variance inflation factor confirms, takes care of the existence of any significant multi-collinearity among the independent variables.

Despite the deletion of Conted_e, the results of the second logit model are similar to the first regression; in fact, the prediction power of Fb_cont (odds ratio) increased slightly to 61 percent. The numbers for the overall goodness-of-fit tests are remarkably high and highly significant for both models. The overall prediction and correct classification level is about 69 percent.

The AIC and SC values indicate a nominally better fit of the first logit model. However, when the AIC and SC numbers for 1991 and 1992 are compared, it can be said that the specified model seemed to be slightly better fitted to the 1991 data.

Based on the statistical results, the overall model (hypothesis 1) can be confirmed. The individual elements that are specified in hypothesis 4 and 8 through 10 can also be confirmed.

Variable:	Probit Model 1: coefficient	Standard error	Probit Model 2: coefficient	standard error
Intercept	-1.8628	.5253	-1.8300	.5140
MGT_QUAL	.0370	.0650	.0370	.0648
REPUT	.0933"	.0485	.1006"	.0482
EMP_QUAL	.0574	.0720	.0476	.0717
PROD_QUL	-.0188	.0780	-.0250	.0777
CONTED_M	-.0747	.1164	-.0714	.0858
CONTED_E	.0045	.1174	omitted	
EXPER	.0185*	.0040	.0187*	.0039
CHG_AVER	.1334"	.0588	.1291"	.0585
FB_CONT	.2806*	.0443	.2912*	.0439
ETH_BEH	.0447	.0521	.0392	.0516
BUSVSFAM	.0191	.0428	.0222	.0422
Likelihood Ratio Chi-Square	1201.28*		1214.41*	
df	942		957	
Pearson Chi-Square	977.58		993.55	
Log Likelihood	-600.64		-607.20	
Note: "p≤.1 ^p≤.01 *p≤.001				

Table 10: Probit Regression Results for INTERSTRATOS 1992

119

The results from the probit regression confirm the findings of the logit model, even to the significance level of the individually significant variables. Also, the overall goodness-of-fit test is highly significant. Based on these results, hypothesis 1, hypothesis 4, and hypotheses 8 through 10 can be confirmed.

4.4.4.3 1993 (IS93)

Variable:	Logit Model 1: coefficient (std. error)	Score Chi-Square	Odds Ratio	Variance Inflation Factor	Logit Model 2: coefficient (std. error)	Score Chi-Square	Odds Ratio	Variance Inflation Factor
Intercept	-3.1198 (1.0730)		.	0	-3.2334 (1.0445))		.	0
MGT_QUAL	-.0122 (.1244)		.988	1.229	.0105 (.1157)		1.011	1.055
REPUT	-.0933 0(.0942)		.911	1.072	-.0928 (.0936)		.911	1.057
EMP_QUAL	.0509 (.1428)		1.052	1.383	omitted			omitted
PROD_QUL	.0821 (.1562)		1.086	1.191	.0992 (.1479)		1.104	1.068
CONTED_M	-.1777 (.2388)		.837	1.884	omitted			omitted
CONTED_E	.4259" (.2401)		1.531	1.909	.3135" (.1776)		1.368	1.048

121

Variable:	Logit Model 1: coefficient (std. error)	Score Chi-Square	Odds Ratio	Variance Inflation Factor	Logit Model 2: coefficient (std. error)	Score Chi-Square	Odds Ratio	Variance Inflation Factor
EXPER	.0087 (.0080)		1.009	1.077	.0084 (.0080)		1.008	1.074
CHG_AVER	.3400^ (.1286)	7.19*	1.405	1.124	.3439^ (.1283)	7.28^	1.410	1.119
FB_CONT	.4099* (.0821)	32.73*	1.507	1.048	.4240* (.0819)	32.90*	1.513	1.044
ETH_BEH	.0490 (.1014)		1.050	1.074	.0551 (.1002)		1.057	1.061
BUSVSFAM	.2669^ (.0853)	10.49*	1.306	1.034	.2683^ (.0852)	10.65*	1.308	1.032
Likelihood Ratio	57.772*				57.614*			
df	11				9			
Lagrange Multiplier	55.414*				55.322*			

Variable:	Logit Model 1: coefficient (std. error)	Score Chi-Square	Odds Ratio	Variance Inflation Factor	Logit Model 2: coefficient (std. error)	Score Chi-Square	Odds Ratio	Variance Inflation Factor
Concordant Predicted Cases	66.1%				66.1%			
Akaike Information Criterion	911.39				912.76			
Schwarz Criterion	915.87				917.25			
Note: ^{a}p≤.1								
^p≤.01								
*p≤.001								

Table 11: Logit Regression Results for INTERSTRATOS 1993

The logit regression analysis of the 1993 data turned up significances for the following individual variables. Conted_e is significant above the 0.1 significance level and Chg_aver above the 0.01 significance level. Most significant are Fb_cont and Busvsfam, which register above the 0.001 significance level. The variables Conted_e and Fb_cont have the highest predictive power, with an odds ratio above 50 percent; while Chg_aver and Busvsfam have predictive power of above 40 percent and above 30 percent, respectively. The stepwise logit regression, then, only confirmed that the exclusion of Conted_e from the stepwise procedure is because its significance level is above 0.1 but not above 0.05.

The tests for multi-collinearity suggested the previously observed (in 1991 and 1992) correlation problem between Conted_e and Conted_m. However, because of the significance of Conted_e, for the second logit model, Conted_m was deleted instead of Conted_e, as followed earlier. Also, for 1993, the variable Emp_qual displayed multi-collinearity with a variance inflation factor of 1.38. And although 1.38 is not greatly in excess of the 30 percent collinearity cut-off point, the variable was dropped from the second logit model.

The second logit model confirmed the general finding of the first model. Conted_e is significant above the 0.1 level, and Chg_aver, Fb_cont and Busvsfam are both significant above the 0.01 level, causing their inclusion in the stepwise logit regression model. The power of prediction of Fb_cont at 51 percent, Chg_aver at 41 percent and Busvsfam at 30 percent remained at about the same magnitude as in the first logit model. Only the odds ratio for Conted_e dropped significantly, that is, to 36.8 percent (from 53.1 percent).

As for the overall model, the two goodness-of-fit tests are both highly significant in both logit models. Their absolute values are identical, almost to the decimal point. The prediction power of the overall model comes in at 66.1 percent of correctly classified cases.

The AIC and SC measure for the comparative specification fit are also almost identical.

Therefore, one can confirm hypothesis 1 for the overall significance of the core model, as well as hypothesis 7, and hypotheses 9, 10 and 12 for the individual core elements.

Variable:	Probit Model 1: coefficient	standard error	Probit Model 2: coefficient	standard error
Intercept	-1.9210	.6585	-1.9933	.6403
MGT_QUAL	-.0098	.0767	.0040	.0715
REPUT	-.0563	.0580	-.0563	.0576
EMP_QUAL	.0315	.0883	omitted	.0915
PROD_QUL	.0508	.0969	.0621	
CONTED_M	-.1113	.1471	omitted	
CONTED_E	.2648"	.1478	.1941"	.1090
EXPER	.0054	.0050	.0052	.0049
CHG_AVER	.2083^	.0765	.2106^	.0763
FB_CONT	.2541*	.0500	.2665*	.0499
ETH_BEH	.0292	.0623	.0331	.0616
BUSVSFAM	.1657^	.0526	.1667^	.0525
Likelihood Ratio Chi-Square	851.46*		853.79*	
df	644		647	
Pearson Chi-Square	654.50		655.79	
Log Likelihood	-425.73		-426.51	

Note: "p≤.1 ^ p≤.01 *p≤.001

Table 12: Probit Regression Results for INTERSTRATOS 1993

The probit regression analysis can basically confirm the results of the logit analysis. Variables Conted_e, Chg_aver, Fb_cont, and Busvsfam come in at high significance levels. Comparatively, only the significance level of Busvsfam drops from above 0.001 in the logit model to above 0.01 in the probit model, while the significance level of the three other variables remain exactly the same. These results are confirmed only in the second probit model inasmuch as multicollinearity was controlled for. The goodness-of-fit test of the overall model, the likelihood ratio chi-square, is highly significant for both probit models. Therefore, hypothesis 1, the hypothesis about the overall model, can be confirmed. In addition, hypotheses 7, 9, 10 and 12 can also be accepted.

4.4.4.4 1994 (IS94)

Variable:	Logit Model 1: coefficient (std. error)	Score Chi-Square	Odds Ratio	Variance Inflation Factor	Logit Model 2: coefficient (std. error)	Score Chi-Square	Odds Ratio	Variance Inflation Factor
Intercept	-1.9631 (1.0163)		.	0	-1.7457 (1.0064)		.	0
MGT_QUAL	-.1294 (.1411)		.879	1.120	-.1331 (.01408)		.875	1.196
REPUT	.2845^ (.0969)	9.61^	1.329	1.128	.2651^ (.0963)	9.59^	1.304	1.120
EMP_QUAL	-.0847 (.1508)		.919	1.253	-.0693 (.1504)		.933	1.250
PROD_QUL	.1898 (.1532)		1.209	1.168	.1802 (.1528)		1.197	1.167
CONTED_M	-.4421" (.2706)		.643	3.144	.0212 (.1523)		1.021	1.040
CONTED_E	.5496" (.2677)		1.732	3.133	omitted			omitted

128

Variable:	Logit Model 1: coefficient (std. error)	Score Chi-Square	Odds Ratio	Variance Inflation Factor	Logit Model 2: coefficient (std. error)	Score Chi-Square	Odds Ratio	Variance Inflation Factor
EXPER	.0051 (.0074)		1.005	1.027	.0053 (.0074)		1.005	1.026
CHG_AVER	.2025" (.1245)		1.224	1.097	.2024" (.1236)		1.224	1.096
FB_CONT	.3380* (.0853)	22.82*	1.402	1.086	.3343* (.0848)	23.02*	1.397	1.086
ETH_BEH	-.0285 (.0980)		.972	1.022	-.0307 (.0976)		.970	1.022
BUSVSFAM	.0048 (.0905)		1.005	1.062	.0028 (.0900)		1.003	1.056
Likelihood Ratio df	44.164* 11				40.117* 10			
Lagrange Multiplier	42.116*				38.555*			

Variable:	Logit Model 1: coefficient (std. error)	Score Chi-Square	Odds Ratio	Variance Inflation Factor	Logit Model 2: coefficient (std. error)	Score Chi-Square	Odds Ratio	Variance Inflation Factor
Concordant Predicted Cases	64.6%				63.7			
Akaike Information Criterion	885.24				887.06			
Schwarz Criterion	889.73				891.54			
Note: "p≤.1 ^p≤.01 *p≤.001								

Table 13: Logit Regression Results for INTERSTRATOS 1994

The results from the first logit regression showed five variables to be significant. The two variables which were confirmed by the stepwise regression as being highly significant are Fb_cont and Reput. The variable Chg_aver was significant above the 0.1 significance level. The next two variables of proposed significance are Conted_m and Conted_e, both with significance levels above 0.1. The odds ratio even suggests that Conted_e by itself accounts for 73.2 percent of the prediction effect.

However, upon closer examination, one finds the variance inflation factor, which is the test for multi-collinearity, to be extraordinarily high for Conted_m and Conted_e; this shows that the earlier suggested effects of these variables are not reliable. Of the three significant individual variables remaining, Fb_cont displays the highest odds ratio, i.e., 40 percent, followed by Reput with a ratio of 33 percent and by Chg_aver with a ratio of 22 percent.

The second logit model excluded the Conted_e variable in an attempt to control multi-collinearity. As the values for the variance inflation factor show, dropping that variable deleted the effects of severe multi-collinearity. The results of the stepwise logit regression show that the most significant and contributing variable is Fb_cont, with a significance level above 0.001. After controlling for multi-collinearity, its odds ratio is at about 40 percent. The second most significant variable is Reput (with a significance level above 0.01), indicating a prediction power of roughly 30 percent through its odds ratio value. The third variable, significant at the 0.1 level, is Chg_aver. It yields a contributing prediction power of 22.4 percent.

The overall measures for the goodness-of-fit test of the model were highly significant for both logit models. The number of correctly classified cases is also quite similar for both models at about 64 percent.

The measures of comparative specification, AIC and SC, are inconclusive in comparing the two logit models. However, they are at their overall lowest for all five years, which suggests that this is the best specified model overall. At the same time, though, the likelihood ratio and the Langrange Multiplier (the goodness-of-fit measures) are also at their comparative low-point, which suggests that these two logit models are not as complete as the other models have been.

Based on these results, the significance of the overall core model can be confirmed (hypothesis 1). In addition, the significance of the following individual variables permits the acceptance of hypotheses 4, 9 and 10.

Variable:	Probit Model 1: coefficient	standard error	Probit Model 2: coefficient	standard error
Intercept	-1.2095	.6251	-1.0824	.6211
MGT_QUAL	-.0806	.0868	-.0807	.0865
REPUT	.1743^	.0596	.1620^	.0591
EMP_QUAL	-.0482	.0922	-.0393	.0919
PROD_QUL	.1141	.0946	.1075	.0944
CONTED_M	-.2758"	.1656	.0130	.0945
CONTED_E	.3437"	.1635	omitted	
EXPER	.0031	.0046	.0033	.0045
CHG_AVER	.1236"	.0747	.1239"	.0742
FB_CONT	.2104*	.0520	.2086*	.0517
ETH_BEH	-.0190	.0600	-.0192	.0600
BUSVSFAM	.0051	.0556	.0038	.0553
Likelihood Ratio Chi-Square	838.62*		844.66*	
df	643		645	
Pearson Chi-Square	650.28		653.37	
Log Likelihood	-419.31		-422.33	

Note: "$p \leq .1$ ^$p \leq .01$ *$p \leq .001$

Table 14: Probit Regression Results for INTERSTRATOS 1994

As with the previous three data sets, the 1994 data set, helps confirm the exact earlier findings of the logit regression. Once the initial model is controlled for multi-collinearity, the number of significant variables reduces from five to three, at the exact same level of significance. The remaining three variables are Reput, Chg_aver and Fb_cont. The test of the goodness-of-fit of the overall model is also highly significant. In summary, the acceptance of hypotheses 1, 4, 9, 10 can be confirmed.

4.4.4.5 1995 (IS95)

Variable:	Logit Model 1: coefficient (std. error)	Score Chi-Square	Odds Ratio	Variance Inflation Factor	Logit Model 2: coefficient (std. error)	Score Chi-Square	Odds Ratio	Variance Inflation Factor
Intercept	-1.2426 (1.0616)	.	.	0	-1.2084 (1.0413)		.	0
MGT_QUAL	.0552 (.1438)		1.057	1.234	.0939 (.1406)		1.098	1.223
REPUT	.3215* (.0960)	12.79"	1.379	1.064	.3337* (.0953)	14.51*	1.396	1.061
EMP_QUAL	-.1002 (.1480)		.905	1.243	-.1313 (.1461)		.877	1.230
PROD_QUL	-.1317 (.1593)		.877	1.149	-.01488 (.1574)		.862	1.140
CONTED_M	-.7565" (.3014)	4.85"	.469	2.944	-.3172" (.1722)		.728	1.019
CONTED_E	.4533 (.2951)		1.573	2.964	omitted			omitted

Variable:	Logit Model 1: coefficient (std. error)	Score Chi-Square	Odds Ratio	Variance Inflation Factor	Logit Model 2: coefficient (std. error)	Score Chi-Square	Odds Ratio	Variance Inflation Factor
EXPER	.0205^ (.0078)	9.09^	1.021	1.044	.0211^ (.0077)	9.18^	1.021	1.042
CHG_AVER	.2294" (.1393)		1.258	1.081	.2178" (.1377)		1.243	1.080
FB_CONT	.4096* (.0871)	30.43*	1.506	1.077	.4292* (.0862)	31.55*	1.536	1.063
ETH_BEH	-.0283 (.0964)		.0972	1.031	-.0503 (.0957)		.951	1.0233
BUSVSFAM	-.0302 (.0860)		.970	1.023	-.0326 (.0850)		.968	1.021
Likelihood Ratio	65.790*				65.165*			
df	11				10			
Lagrange Multiplier	62.419*				61.850*			
Concordant Predicted Cases	66.6%				66.5%			

Variable:	Logit Model 1: coefficient (std. error)	Score Chi-Square	Odds Ratio	Variance Inflation Factor	Logit Model 2: coefficient (std. error)	Score Chi-Square	Odds Ratio	Variance Inflation Factor
Akaike Information Criterion	906.75				920.21			
Schwarz Criterion	911.23				924.72			
Note: 'p≤.1 ^p≤.01 *p≤.001								

Table 15: Logit Regression Results for INTERSTRATOS 1995

The results from the logit regression with the data set from the final year (1995), turned out with the highest number of individually significant variables. The five variables of Reput, Conted_m, Exper, Chg_aver, and Fb_cont are reported significantly in the first logit model.

The stepwise logit regression indicates Fb_cont to have the highest explanatory power, followed by Reput, Exper and Conted_m. Only Chg_aver was not reported when the significance threshold was increased to 0.05. Regarding the odds ratio Fb-cont turned out to have the highest prediction power (50.6%), followed by Reput with 37.9 percent, and Chg_aver with 25.8 percent. Conted_e also displayed a high odds ratio, but the variable was not significant, and moreover a high degree of correlation with Conted_m seems prevalent.

In the second logit model Conted_e was eliminated for suspicion of causing multi-collinearity. With the omission of Conted_e no further evidence of multi-collinearity surfaced.

As in the first logit model, the second logit model as well produces high significances for the same five variables. The stepwise regression confirms the earlier results, and only omits Conted_m from selection through its 0.05 threshold. This may indicate that the earlier level of significance of Conted_m, is partially caused by correlation with Conted_e. Nevertheless after correcting for multi-collinearity, the five variables of Reput, Conted_m, Exper, Chg_aver, and Fb_cont remain significant and included in the model. The highest explanatory power is again with Fb_cont, with an increased odds ratio of 53.6 percent, followed by Reput with 39.6 percent and Chg_aver at 24.3 percent. And while Conted_m is a significant variable, its odds ratio is not an individually contributing predictor.

The measures of the overall model and goodness-of-fit test are highly significant for both indicators, and are hardly distinguishable for the first or second logit model. Equally similar is the percentage of correctly classified cases, which is about 66.6 percent.

The comparative model specification tests of AIC and SC slightly favor the first model. Combining the goodness-of-fit tests, with the percentage of correctly classified cases and the comparative model specification test, the logit models for the 1995 data set seem to produce the overall best results. The goodness-of-fit tests display relatively high values, with the percentage of concordant predictions also being rather high, and the AIC and SC values also being at a comparatively good low.

Based on these logit regression results, the significance of the overall model can be confirmed (hypothesis 1). In addition, the significance of the five individual variables permits the acceptance of hypotheses 4, 6, 8, 9, 10.

Variable:	Probit Model 1: coefficient	standard error	Probit Model 2: coefficient	standard error
Intercept	-.7652	.6499	-.7448	.6378
MGT_QUAL	.0352	.0888	.0593	.0869
REPUT	.1992*	.0592	.2062*	.0586
EMP_QUAL	-.0653	.0907	-.0839	.0896
PROD_QUL	-.0812	.0975	-.0928	.0964
CONTED_M	-.4696^	.1834	-.1977"	.1057
CONTED_E	.2810	.1794	omitted	
EXPER	.0129^	.0048	.0132^	.0047
CHG_AVER	.1388"	.0830	.1334"	.0824
FB_CONT	.2571*	.0533	.2688*	.0527
ETH_BEH	-.0181	.0590	-.0310	.0586
BUSVSFAM	-.0188	.0527	-.0196	.0521
Likelihood Ratio Chi-Square	838.20*		852.36*	
df	645		655	
Pearson Chi-Square	648.54		658.18	
Log Likelihood	-419.10		-426.18	

Note: "$p \leq .1$ ^ $p \leq .01$ *$p \leq .001$

Table 16: Probit Regression Results for INTERSTRATOS 1995

The results of the probit regression for 1995, are much like all the previous years, concordant with the results from the logit regression. The variables of Reput, Conted_m, Exper, Chg_aver, and Fb_cont are all highly significant, even assuming the same level of significance as in the logit model. The test for the overall goodness-of-fit of the model comes in also highly significant, and the measurable effects of multi-collinearity (or controlling for it, for that matter) are negligible.

The results permit the acceptance of the overall significant core model (hypothesis 1), along with the significant individual variables, confirming hypotheses 4, 6, 8, 9, and 10.

4.4.4.6 Summary of significant results

The table below summarizes the most significant elements of each annual analysis.

In conclusion it can be said that the logit and probit models for each year were highly significant, and neither model seemed greatly better suited than the other.

Hypothesis 2 could in the end also be confirmed, as it suggested that the overall core model would not change over time, as indicated through the continuos significance of each complete yearly model.

Hypotheses 1, 9 and 10 were the only hypotheses that could be confirmed for each of the years. However, only hypotheses 3, 5, 11 and 13 could not be confirmed for any year.

In the final chapter a discussion and interpretation of these results will ensue.

Year: (Data set)	Significant Variables:	Logit Likelihood Ratio:	Correctly Predicted Cases:	Probit Likelihood Ratio Chi-Square:	Hypotheses Confirmed:
1991 (IS91)	Exper, Chg_aver, Fb_cont	81*	66%	1100*	H1, H8, H9, H10
1992 (IS92)	Reput, Exper, Chg_aver, Fb_cont	110*	69%	1200*	H1, H4, H8, H9, H10
1993 (IS93)	Conted_e, Chg_aver, Fb_cont, Busvsfam	57*	66%	850*	H1, H7, H9, H10, H12
1994 (IS94)	Reput, Chg_aver, Fb_cont	42*	64%	840*	H1, H4, H9, H10
1995 (IS95)	Reput, Conted_m, Exper, Chg_aver, Fb_cont	62*	66%	845*	H1, H4, H6, H8, H9, H10
Overall:	Chg_aver, Fb_cont	scores >42 and <110, all highly significant	all predictions >64% (and < 69%)	all chi-square ratios highly significant (>840 and <1200)	H1, H2, H9, H10

(*p≤.001)

Table 17: Comparative Significance Statistics 1991-1995

143

5. DISCUSSION

> Stride for perfection;
> realizing nothing is created
> in completion, with every
> day one approaches
> perfection...
> (Baltasar Gracian SJ,
> 1647[305])

In this final chapter, the first section (5.1) will be a presentation of the refined, contextually sensitized model of the family business core; the following sections will be further elaborations on the major individual conjectures. Within the context of this refined model, the results from the statistical analysis will be interpreted (5.2). The concluding section of this research will be a discussion of this research's shortcomings (5.3), implications for future research (5.4) and a summary with concluding questions (5.5).

5.1 The refined model

While the general model suggested earlier (cf. Figure 6: Family business core, periphery and environment, page 94) and the conjectures in it still retain validity, the core elements which were previously introduced in a merely descriptive fashion (cf. Figure 7: Family business core elements, page 95) will now be refined. The proposed core elements of family business are now put in context, and their process interaction will be explained. In the terminology of grounded theory, the over-arching categories which were determined in the first stage of this research are now integrated in a process model[306].

For a graphical depiction of the refined core model of family business see Figure 8.

---

[305] "Hombre en su punto. No se nace hecho; vase de cada dia perficionado..." Gracian, 1992, No. 6:2; translation by this author
[306] cf. Strauss & Corbin, 1990

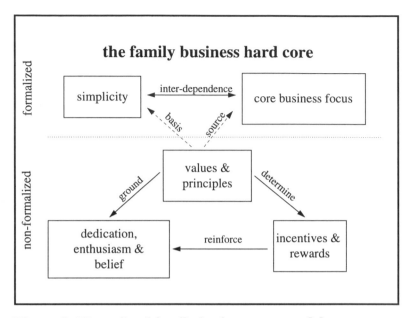

Figure 8: The refined family business core model

This refined core model of family business as a organizational form is the process model which evolved and was developed from the collected empirical data.

This model has five core elements. The first division of the core elements is between those elements which can be termed *formalized* and those which can be termed *non-formalized*. The formalized core elements, *viz.* simplicity and core business focus, are the applied side of the core. These elements are used in the operation of the business and are in some way concrete and perceivable, sometimes even quantifiable. The non-formal core elements, however, are of a more abstract sort, because they are not directly linked to the business. They are asserted to be the underlying, driving force of the organization, yet a quantitative count will most certainly be impossible. One conceivable reason why these elements cannot be formalized is the fact that all or some of the components are not in the awareness of the organization and/or its members. Hence, often times the detection and determination of these elements is feasible only through the emanation of these core elements in actions or through similarly observable processes.

Another way of thinking about the distinction between the formalized and non-formalized elements, is by means of the dichotomy of business and

146

society. The formalized elements are most likely to surface as part of the business system, whereas the non-formalized elements are part of the larger, societal system.

Now, at the center of this core model are the values and principles of an organization. Descriptions and examples of them were given in the previous subsections[307]. It should be stressed that these values and principles are theorized to be imprinted during the organization's birth and to subsequently remain unchanged.

These values and principles, then, serve to ground the dedication, enthusiasm and belief of the organization. Inasmuch as these values are considered to be of a higher level of abstraction, the dedication component can be viewed as an application or grounding of these values and principles. Consequently, the relationship of these more abstract elements to the more concrete ones can and must be understood only as unidirectional and not as interactional.

In a similar way, the values and principles of an organization determine the kind and quantity of the incentives and rewards. Similarly, too, the incentives are a somewhat concretized, applied aspect of the values. What is different, though, in the case of the dedication elements is that values serve as intrinsic motivators for the organizational agent, while the incentives serve as a system's internal feedback for adequate dedication, enthusiasm and belief, in addition to an inherent process view. This essentially is also the explanation of how the incentives reinforce the dedication core component.

On the formalized side of the model, it is proposed that the values and principles serve as the ground for simplicity and the core business focus. Note, however, the proposed inter-dependence between the simplicity category and core business focus category: these elements serve as an internal validation system in that each must be in check for the other to adequately function.

---

[307] cf. section 4.3 on page 95

In conclusion, it must be stated that, although every core aspect originates from the values and principles core component, and as such are uni-directional and non-looped, the system as a whole represents an externally looped feedback system. That means what keeps this subsystem in check is the necessity for overall equilibration in the larger system. As explained briefly earlier, the system cannot work if any component and its subsequent connections are out of balance, or over- or under-developed in relation to the other components. This externalized check not only serves the function of demonstrating the importance of the congruence and embeddedness of this system vis-à-vis the larger system or environment, but it also exhibits how core changes are possible, i.e. through revolutionary changes in the larger system, which would serve to immediately un-balance the existing core system, and lead either to its abandonment or to radical adaptation.

Whereas the above section served to define the refined model and the terms for the interaction between the model's core elements, the following section focuses on a detailed explanation of the individual core components.

5.1.1 Simplicity

Although the model proposed in this research is original in its total construction, it makes use of terms and concepts used in previous research. In particular, the term *simplicity* and the term *core focus* have been used rather recently to refer to characteristics vital to the successful continuation of organizations[308].

Although the use of the term simplicity in reports of earlier research can be viewed as detracting from the absolute originality of the construct called simplicity in this research, it can also be considered to have the compensating effect of validating the emergence in this research of the category which is also called *simplicity*; in this way, the earlier research can be seen as adding credibility to the overall model of the present research. From this point of view, it could be even said that 'simplicity simplifies'.

As mentioned above, the construct or category called *simplicity* has appeared rather recently in the literature. In particular, Rommel et al.

---

[308] Rommel et al., 1995; Simon, 1996

identify (in their study of German firms) successful firms as those which focus on what the researchers call simplicity (and quality)[309]. This is quite in contrast to some other organizational research that postulates the need of explaining firms' behavior with the construct or category that is termed complexity[310]. This example of such earlier research is given both to demonstrate that there is no coherence in the progression of the organization field from research to research and also to point out that both simplicity and complexity references are polarities of yet another continuum. In this present research, the different and more abstract meaning of simplicity which is proper to the evolutionary ecology model of family business will be explained and utilized.

It is important to bear in mind that the terms simplicity and complexity used in earlier research to refer to the polarities of a continuum were terms used within the context of organizational theory. In the context of (organizational) fieldwork and grounded theory development, on the other hand, the term simplicity (or simple) refers to a construct or category of a somewhat different meaning. Simplicity refers in the usage of these organizations not to some simple-mindedness of an organization's members, but rather to the ability of an organization as such to make simple sense of a complex environment. Simplicity refers to the aptitude for realizing and recognizing what is essential; a concrete expression of this aptitude, of this simplicity, is the observable avoidance of, or verbalized aversion to, following whatever management fad or wave comes along.

Although this sense-making of an organization – very much in the Weickian sense of the term[311] – is usually facilitated through the person and institution of the entrepreneur, it can function and find concrete expression in other observable ways and thus should always be understood as a characteristic or property of the organization as such, hence it should not be confused with or reduced to either a personality trait of an individual member of the

---

[309] Rommel et al., 1995

[310] Covin & Slevin, 1997:103; Kauffman, 1993; Kauffman, 1995; McKelvey, 1996; Stacey, 1995

[311] Weick, 1995

organization or to any composite or aggregate of such individual traits of the members.

It would indeed be a mistake to repeat errors made during the early parts of the evolution of entrepreneurship research by now attempting to list characteristics or traits this person or institution needs to possess[312]. Rather, this grounded theory simply abstracts from descriptive observation and does not claim to have any predictive ability.

This will be explained in part later on, but for now suffice it to say that a pattern emerged from the observations of this empirical research which corresponds to, and confirms the existence of, the process of initial imprinting which had been assumed by earlier researchers such as Stinchcombe and later McKelvey[313]. To assume the existence of such a process of organizational imprinting may seem to imply a rather blunt determinism, but this process can be explained in a different way – namely, as an interdependence of selection and adaptation, as was suggested earlier and will be explained later in more detail[314].

Another reason why the element of simplicity should not be classified as a personality trait is that the element called individual sense-making – or in epistemological terms, social construction – deserves to be recognized. That is to say that, while simplicity may well appear to be clear and obvious to the trained observer of an organization, the members actively carrying out their roles in that same organization may not recognize the phenomenon being explained here by the concept of simplicity, or if they do recognize the phenomenon, may disagree with the kind of explanation proposed. Implied here again is the contention that there is in a successful organization an operative process of sense-making and hence the potential of so doing called simplicity regardless of whether or not anyone inside or outside of that organization is aware of the process or accepts any of the proposed explanations for it, such as some sort of birth imprinting process.

---

[312] cf. for example Low & MacMillan, 1988; "It seems that any attempt to profile the typical entrepreneur is inherently futile" (p. 148)

[313] McKelvey, 1982; Stinchcombe, 1965

[314] cf. page 163

Simplicity leads to, and is recursively connected back from, the second core element, focus on core business, by suggesting that extensive product (or service) diversification intuitively runs counter to simplicity.

5.1.2 Focus on core business

As mentioned in the introductory sentence to sub-section 5.1.1 above, the issue of focus on core business has only recently been taken up by organizational researchers. In a recent study, Simon determined that among the distinguishing elements of successful, market-dominating German businesses (mostly small or medium-sized family-owned businesses) a distinct focus on one or two product lines or services was prevalent[315]. A whole other line of inquiry determined that an organization's competitiveness and future success were completely dependent on its core competencies and their development, implying a focus on a single-product-line and running counter to the trend of the 1980's which suggested diversification together with mergers and acquisitions[316].

The most developed argument, however, is that of Simon who determined that a firm's continuing success was not due to a cyclical change in strategic focus, but rather because of a fixed focus on a maximum of two product-lines during the life span of such an organization[317].

This very phenomenon that Simon described was also found within the organizations involved in this research, where the prevalent approach was the two-tiered product line[318]. But again what is important in this research is not simply that this core business focus existed in these organizations, but rather that there existed a prior and continued commitment to this core business. Once again, the commitment of the firms to the core business did not come about with the rise of the latest management fad, but was evident in the initial evolutionary process of these organizations.

---

[315] Simon, 1996

[316] Hamel & Prahalad, 1994; Lorange, 1995; March & Sproull, 1990; Moore, 1993; Pfeffer, 1994; Seidel, 1995

[317] Simon, 1996

[318] cf. Table 4 on page 93

Now, some critics will argue that by itself a focus on one or two product lines, or even on geographical regions (for that matter), is not a function of some family business's superior ability, but rather a function of firm size. While this argument has an initial appeal, it rather quickly becomes evident that this counter-argument is no argument at all. Given the fact that the firms in question are market leaders – whether their market be defined by product niche and/or geographical region – it can be safely assumed that sustainable market leadership is accompanied by some form of profitability. And even while the current employment size might be limited to its current status – that is market domination could only be marginally extended – the assumption of financial profitability would permit the firm to grow and enter into new markets and/or products, if this were desirable. Hence, it must be concluded that firm size is not the determinant of core business focus, but is rather the result of the firm's voluntary decision.

Lastly, another issue deserving emphasis is that of perception and social construction. What the outside observer may determine to be a smart strategic positioning in one or two product lines might not be perceived in the same way by the entrepreneur or the organization. Put differently, the positioning of product lines may be a conscious decision made by the organization, however, it is also quite imaginable that this is the result of a slow product-related evolutionary process, such as the interplay between long-term decision making and market driven product selection and survival. More abstractly, path dependence and history observance retain validity when applied to the core business foci.

5.1.3 Dedication, enthusiasm and belief

Since the early research on entrepreneurship, the elements of dedication, enthusiasm and belief have been mentioned in one form or another in regard to the relationship of the entrepreneur to his/her business[319]. So, in one sense, the proposition that these elements are existent and important core features may seem trivial. However, if one imagines, for example, a large diversified multi-national conglomerate formed in the 1980's being

---

[319] cf. Sexton & Kasarda, 1992; Sexton & Smilor, 1997 for multiple and manifold references

informed by its consultants in the 1990's that it needs to further develop its core competencies, re-focus its business, and purge itself of its diversified holdings, then it is hard to imagine that such a firm could undertake such a transformation without also having to re-focus its elements of dedication, enthusiasm and belief. This example serves to emphasize the vital importance of this seemingly trivial, perhaps even obvious, fact. It also emerged from observation that dedication, enthusiasm and belief are all qualitative elements which increase significantly in strength and credibility as the organization grows in maturity.

Without intending to overemphasize this one component, it may safely be said here that a family firm's dedication to, enthusiasm for, and belief in, the business appeared to emerge as the strongest single core feature characterizing the successful family business. These elements were not observed as glib self-descriptions of such a business, and in fact were rarely ever verbalized, but as impressively lived-out characteristics and emanating motivators, which refreshingly contrasted with the "I just work here"-attitude, so often prevalent in large non-family-owned corporate settings.

After this phenomenon was observed, the question arose as to what triggered and motivated this dedicated behavior. Answers appeared to surface in the two remaining core elements.

5.1.4 Values and principles

Categorically separate, yet contextually inseparable from dedication, enthusiasm and belief are the values and principles animating the family business core.

While some detailed values and principles were delineated in the conjectures section, this is not the place for lists, but rather for expressly articulating what is meant in this context by values and principles.

It may be stated without hesitation that among the participating family businesses in the five European countries, no single overarching or generally acceptable principle or value could be determined. Therefore, the argument made here for the necessity of core values is an argument not for any specific values or principles, but merely for the existence of values and principles in general.

Consequently, the construct is that the existence of deeply rooted values and principles serves as one discriminator between the more successful family firms and the less successful ones. At a higher level of abstraction, this argument could be extended to apply to all forms of successful-versus-unsuccessful organizational forms.

It needs to be emphasized again that not the content but the valid presence and permanence are the proposed vital substance.

Values and principles can be expressed in many specific forms. A written document would be the least expected. These elements could be transposed into legacies, lived-out models, generally held codes of behavior, or any other form of conscious or unconscious purpose.

Values and principles are not, for example, recently formulated mission statements, mission statements initiated by some fickle management fashion; no, they are values and principles imprinted at the origin and inception of the organization.

5.1.5 Incentives and rewards

The last of the five core elements is the element called incentives and rewards. This element, too, is inter-connected as a motivator with the element called dedication, enthusiasm and belief. Incentives and rewards comprise the least abstract element of the core, and serve as an indispensable link within the core model. They are important because they represent the concrete results of positive feedback to desired modes of behavior. They do not serve as ultimately satisfying objectives, but are necessary to maintain the interaction between values and dedication.

There are two issues which can be outlined in a more abstract fashion in this section without being supported by contextual examples.

First, the exact and actual nature of the incentives and rewards is irrelevant. What is important is not their material character, but a consistent and logically congruent system of rewarding organization members. Hence, no immediate qualitative difference is claimed for either a stock option plan or a periodic family business picnic.

Second, although the existence of incentives and rewards is important, of greater significance is the equilibration among these three elements, values, dedication and rewards. Proportions and relationship strengths must be in synch for this sub-system to function well. For example, big rewards will ultimately do little for an organization, if dedication is non-existent. Conversely, the greatest values and resultant enthusiasm will result in nothing less than failure if no feedback loop in the form of incentives is provided.

5.2 Validation of the refined model through INTERSTRATOS

In chapter four a derivation of the hypotheses based on the proposed elements of the family business core was presented, and logit and probit regressions were modeled to test those hypotheses, with the significant results displayed in the tables:

The most significant results of the regression tests were (a) the confirmation of the existence of a family business core, as proposed in the model and also (b) the confirmation of the stability of the core model over a five year period. The majority of hypotheses about individual core elements were confirmed, at least during one year, with only three hypotheses proving significant for every year (H1, H9, H10) and four hypothesis proving insignificant for each year (H3, H5, H11, H13).

The interpretation of the individual results of this statistical analysis are as follows.

Hypothesis 1 sought to test for the existence and distinguishability of a family business core. Since this hypothesis was strongly confirmed, the inference can be drawn that the specified core of the family business exists and furthermore is distinct from non-family business. However, because of the structure of the data, it cannot be said whether non-family businesses have a different core, or simply do not possess a distinguishable core at all. Nevertheless, for the purposes of this investigation, it was important to determine that the modeled family business core exists and is specifiable and is therefore detectable. Naturally, the limitations on the strength of the constructed proxies still apply.

In hypothesis 2 the existence of a distinguishable family business core (which was proposed and subsequently confirmed in hypothesis 1) was assumed and it was sought to be tested whether or not this family business core remained stable over time. The INTERSTRATOS data set permitted monitoring of the core over a five year period. In the theoretical explanation it was proposed that the idea of such a family business core would make sense only if it remained stable over time, hence with the confirmation of hypothesis 2 the validity of this theoretical construct was emphasized. With the limitations of the data and the proxy construction in mind, the important purpose of confirming this hypothesis was to indicate the lack of any change or disintegration of the core. Hence, the confirmation of the tendency of a stable core is sufficient validation for this theoretical construct of core stability. Also, it was never claimed or intended that confirming this hypothesis would prove that the core consisted, for example, of 20 percent element A at time 1 and would contain an equal amount at time 2.

In addition to the hypotheses having overall significance, namely, hypotheses 1 and 2 – hypotheses 9 and 10 were the only hypotheses concerning the individual core elements that were continuously significant for all five years.

Hypothesis 9 was intended to test whether or not family businesses were more likely to value the avoidance of change than non-family businesses. The wording of this question in the questionnaire does not imply that avoidance has any positive or negative connotation, nor does it imply the significance of the change. Hence, through the confirmation of hypothesis 9, it is argued that avoidance of change *per se* is a positive quality inherent in the family business. It means that family businesses are able to keep their focus on the core business and also are signaling a preference for maintaining simplicity. However, it cannot be inferred from this answer how family businesses distinguish between change, only that the core business focus is not easily put in dis-equilibrium. Stated directly, this hypothesis suggests that change by itself is not something family businesses aspire to or value highly, and upon reflection one would hope that this more contemplative view would prevail, as change should be a means, and not an end to organizational goals. However, this finding does not suggest that family businesses are unable or unwilling to change. Put in concrete terms, this probably means that family businesses are less likely to fall for the next management consultancy fad, and prefer keeping things simple and therefore in perspective – in the perspective of their core business.

Hypothesis 10 tested whether or not family businesses believed that their firm should remain in family hands. The result suggests that family businesses would prefer to stay in family hands. And while to some extent this outcome might seem to have been easily predictable, it is only predictable insofar as a preference for retaining its organizational form is assumed. Otherwise it is not so clear why the entrepreneurs and owners of other medium-sized firms would explicitly not want the firm to stay in family hands.

It would be expected that concern for the value of family ownership would decrease as firm size, with the attendant growth in number and diversity of stockholders, would increase. To be clear the result does not suggest that family businesses want to keep the firm in family hands at all cost, endangering the health of the firm. Rather one interpretation of this hypothesis confirmation could be that the keeping of the firm in family hands is a pro-active decision on the firm's part, indicating their value for this life system – a system (a way of life, their vocation) of rewards and incentives for building, maintaining and expanding the firm. And by placing emphasis on maintaining the firm in family hands the system is kept in balance, and therefore provides for the future, emphasizing again the long-term perspective. As indicated earlier, it is not quite clear why other entrepreneurs would not care to maintain the firm in family hands, and therefore with this result it can be assumed that this care and value for maintaining the firm in family hands is an element that distinguishes family businesses from non-family businesses. Also, by indicating the desire to keep the firm in family hands, the ability to simplify is emphasized once more, as this desire is also what can be called a planned exit strategy.

Hypotheses 4, 6, 7, 8 and 12 were confirmed at least once during the five years. Despite the fact that these five hypotheses could not be confirmed for all five years, the variables they presented were nonetheless of significant value to the overall model for all five years, thus warranting inclusion. However, one can only speculate why these variables did not produce significant results over all five years.

Hypothesis 4 was confirmed in three of the five years. The hypothesis tested for the importance of a firm's reputation, and the results suggest that family businesses seem to place a higher value on firm reputation than non-family businesses. The underlying variable was used as a proxy for the existence of values and principles as a core element of family businesses.

Hypotheses 6 and 7 tested for the importance of continuing education for management and employees. Both hypotheses could only be confirmed in one year. The value of continuing education was suggested to imply the existence of a system of motivators, incentives and rewards, as the employer and employee would mutually gain from the availability of such program.

Hypothesis 8 tested whether the entrepreneur at the helm of a family firm would have more years of experience than the non-family business entrepreneur. It would seem reasonable to believe that since entrepreneurship is probably a roughly equal choice for the family business entrepreneur and the non-family business entrepreneur, a significant difference in associating with one firm would mean greater dedication to the family firm. Hypothesis 8 could only be confirmed for three of five years.

Hypothesis 12 tested whether the family business entrepreneur was distinct from the non-family business entrepreneur in prioritizing business affairs over family life. Since this hypothesis could only be confirmed for one year, it suffices to mention in passing that the activity of prioritizing was suggested to be a proxy for the existence of values.

Hypotheses 3, 5, 11 and 13 could not be confirmed for any of the five years for which data was available. Hypotheses 3 and 5 stressed the importance of the quality of management and the quality of employees, respectively. The findings do not suggest that there is no value attributed by entrepreneurs and managers to quality management and/or employees; rather the findings imply only that the importance of management and employee quality is not a factor which distinguishes family businesses from non-family businesses. One might assume that the questions might have been too generic for any significant differences to develop.

Hypothesis 11 tested for the value of the importance of ethical behavior. No significant difference in valuing ethics between family businesses and non-family businesses could be found. Perhaps, an item like ethical behavior could be better tested in a more indirect way, such as ranking of possible behaviors in contingent situations. However, because of the general phrasing in the questionnaire, no difference in ethical values could be determined.

Hypothesis 13 tested for the importance placed on product quality. And here also no significant difference was found between the family business and non-family business responses. One might suspect that the public opinion of the issues represented by these four proven insignificant items was too skewed, for these general questions to detect and measure a significant difference between family businesses and non-family businesses. Especially, the issue of valuing ethical behavior warrants possible future investigation since it could be hypothesized that in a developed long-term focused system, such as a family business, the emphasis on, awareness of and need for ethical behavior could be expected to be higher than in non-family firms.

In summary, the overall results from the statistical analysis corroborate the findings of the qualitative data analysis, namely, the proposed core model of family business. The logit and probit models for all five years were very robust and thus satisfactory. However, as was mentioned earlier in detail, the construction of individual proxies was only through single items, and most of the single items themselves yielded possible multiple interpretations. Therefore, future research could attempt to construct multiple item scales to validate hypotheses in addition to more clearly phrased questionnaire items, which would fortify these findings to an even greater extent. Despite the weak individual proxies, the robustness of the overall model and the consistency of findings for all five years gives considerable validity and authority to the overall model, thus realizing the main goal proposed for this research.

5.3 Caveats

On a formal level there are many limitations to a rather extensive study like this one. However, the rationale, for example, for choosing five countries was explained in the methodology chapter, and for those reasons a suggestion for the inclusion of additional countries seems unnecessary, if not down right redundant at this point.

Instead, the purpose of this section is to reflect on the macro level issues, such as the overall sufficiency and achievement of the set goals.

In epistemological terms this study vindicates the utilization of multi-tiered methodological approaches. The utilization of multiple methods can help bring out the strength of the individual methodological steps in a synergistic fashion. And while general advancement of triangulation methodologies and multi-method approaches is advocated, it should, however, not be made an end in itself.

Another limitation is the lack of perfect synchronization between the qualitative data results and the questionnaire design of the quantitative data. Ideally, the questionnaire should have been designed on the basis of the results of the qualitative data analysis. However, two reasons prevented the collection of longitudinal quantitative data based on the qualitatively derived model. First, the INTERSTRATOS data had already been collected and was readily available for this study. Secondly, the estimated costs associated with collecting quantitative longitudinal data from a variety of countries on the basis of the qualitative data were beyond the consideration and reach of this study, especially in light of the existence of the rather adequate INTERSTRATOS data set. This fact illuminates the financial and other constraints on carrying out (future) combinatory research.

It should be noted again that, because of the imperfect synchronization between the qualitative model and the quantitative data utilized for validation, the proxies constructed for the model validation were sufficient, yet in general considerations rather weak.

In addition to the call for multi-item scales and validation, future quantitative research on family business could also benefit from the inclusion of information on generational status.

160

Also, this study utilized conjectures from a distinct, more mature research program (organizational ecology), and consequently it can be said that this strategy for the building and advancement of family business theory was sufficiently successful. Hence, for further theory development, the utilization of other such theories ought to be considered by other researchers. Concerted efforts of this sort of theory building are evident in entrepreneurship, where, for example, conjectures from economics and sociology are examined and considered[320].

Regarding the refined core model, it was stated that the model claims to have no predictive power and yet intends to be a integral model. This apparent contradiction can be viewed in different ways. From an epistemological point of view, this is a clash between the assumptions of the positivist and the social constructivist. The positivist asserts that if a model claims to explain the past and present of a certain setting, it must have predictive power, otherwise it is merely a poor model. The social constructivist, however, is concerned, not with predicting, but with understanding the multiplicity of the present.
Consequently, as regards its application, this study is of little value to the person designing public policy since no authoritative, predictive statements are even intended. However, the person interested in comprehending the detailed internal processes of the evolution of a family business may take away useful insights.

So in instances where a concrete application is sought, or a specific problem solution is needed, a different kind of model is needed. For example, Alden Lank's family business role theory is such a situational example (cf. Figure 9). By viewing the family business and its parts in different roles, concrete problems – such as inter-generational conflicts – can be assessed and solved, however, one would not want to claim that such a model can help in the understanding of the evolution of family business as an organizational form.

---

[320] cf. especially the book by Bull, Thomas & Willard, 1995, but also Bull & Willard, 1993; Bygrave, 1990a; Bygrave, 1990b; Bygrave, 1993

The above distinction between different ways in which a theory can be useful is by no means intended to be judgmental; on the contrary, it illuminates the fact that there is suitability and applicability for more than one theory and one kind of theory.

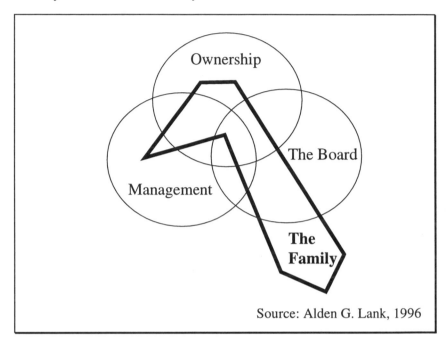
Source: Alden G. Lank, 1996

Figure 9: The "Family Business Tie"

5.4 Future research

This research provides an evolutionary model of family business ecology – as a distinct organizational form – based on grounded theory. In line with the demands of the grounded theory approach, future research must attempt to validate, refute or refine the model presented in this research. Different settings will need different models. However, an accumulation of these studies should exponentially increase understanding of the family business as an organizational form as these theoretical models become more dense and comprehensive.

A positivist, of course, will question the validity and usefulness of increasing efforts to understand family business and model a general theory, without deriving immediate prescriptive benefits from it.

Also, it makes sense to call for more longitudinal research on family business. So, a call for action seems warranted to collect such mostly qualitative information from family businesses over the decades to come inasmuch as family businesses by nature are characterized by the involvement of multiple generations.

With the understanding that the model of family business presented here is context specific and is, therefore, in some sense incomplete, it would be best to direct future research toward increasing theoretical density of the model before attempting the operationalization of core elements. This is not to say, however, that operationalization cannot be done; exemplars of operationalizations were used in this research for the regression analysis of the INTERSTRATOS data.

On the theoretical level, most pressing and most in need for attention seems to be the question of what happens in the initial stage of family business development and why. And while that question is important, conceivably it is hard to determine a sound way to propose a research agenda for the matter, as is evident from the total lack of research in the area for decades. However, as progress is made in this process and insights result from it, certain phenomena which up to now have either been neglected or explained away merely as some kind of imprinting will hopefully be better understood.

5.5 Summary and concluding questions

The purpose of this final section of this last chapter is to outline the major findings of this research.

Medium-sized family businesses were observed in their actions and their responses to the formation of the European Union. Although the political process of forming the European Union is and was rather gradual, no drastic or rash actions were taken by these family businesses in response to this changing environment. Based on this analysis, it is concluded that for these family businesses there was a sense-making process going on – consciously or unconsciously – that suggested the necessity for some adaptation, i.c., the re-framing of their context – their mental imaging or cognitive mapping, if you will. However, a selection process was also exerting its power, hence not giving the family businesses every choice; a selection dynamic such as

163

the imposition of the new super-infrastructure of the European Union, along with its institutional rules. Thus, if a single answer had to be provided to the question of what family businesses did in response to the European Union, it would have to be that family businesses engaged in retrospective sense-making[321], leading them to some (cognitive) actions on the individual level, and realizations on an aggregate (population) level, hence combining selection and adaptation views. Conceptually, the most adequate view of this phenomenon seems to be Weick's proposition that every individual (or entity) creates its own individual environment, thereby uniting selection and adaptation views[322].

Thus, from a theoretical perspective this research suggests that, in its extreme, the dichotomy between adaptation and selection is not very helpful in explaining change behavior, and thus adaptation and selection should be viewed instead as interdependent.

This research also devised a model of the family business core, based on a grounded theory analysis. This core model explains the organizational form of family business as a holistic system with a long-term perspective. This system-based view permits the observation and analysis of the evolution of family business. However, the presented core model has no predictive intent or capacity, because it is mainly argued that for prediction to become a sensible task, a deep and thorough understanding of the phenomenon must first be established. This core model is viewed as such a necessary first step. Also, this research never intended to provide how-to solutions to operational problems of family business, but rather provide a theoretical vehicle to holistically conceptualize family businesses.

While the form of family business is distinguishable from other organizational forms, a natural advantage of family businesses is its long-time perspective, allowing researchers to study evolution without much of the 'noise' that accompanies many of the other organizational forms. To be more specific, the proposed core model of family business focuses on the individual core elements and their interaction without, however, having to

---

[321] in the Weickian sense, cf. Weick, 1995:24
[322] cf. Weick, 1995:167

specify the actions of agents because it is assumed that family business is a closed and looped system, entailing equilibration of all elements.

To better illustrate this point, two negative examples, i.e., non-family business examples will be used. First, take the example of IBM. After a prolonged crisis and stalemate, Louis Gerstner was hired from an outside firm to become the new CEO of IBM in 1993. According to various sources, IBM had a very distinct culture, which one would assume were based on its values and core. Since the arrival of the new CEO, many changes took place and the firm re-gained financial profitability. However, this particular evolutionary process could not be clearly distinguished because bringing in an outsider caused 'noise', that is, it is unknown whether the evolution of the firm was based on the original values and core of the firm, or whether the new CEO basically created new values and a core, or whether the evolution was the interplay of the old core and the new CEO's values. The point of this example is that family businesses have a natural advantage in their lack of noise and exogenous shocks, which means that research can be done on evolutionary processes without the need for reductionism.

The example of Intel and its recently retired CEO, Andy Groves, corroborates this last point. With western capital markets demanding short-term profitability, the average reign of any one CEO is perhaps a mere 5 to 10 years. Conceivably, then, the reign of Mr. Groves might abruptly end with the failure of the next Intel computer chip. Therefore, with a new CEO, it can only be assumed that the future course of the firm and its consequences will occur because of the past CEO, despite the past CEO or regardless of the past CEO.

Clearly, there are some (mostly immediate) benefits to the stakeholders of these firms. However, if research is to gain new insights into the evolutionary processes of organizations, a more stable, long-term-oriented setting is appropriate and seems warranted. Because the organizational form of family business by definition entails such stability and long-term orientation, it is an attractive, natural setting for the study of the evolutionary processes in question. Hence, the natural setting of family business can serve as a foundation for the study of these evolutionary change processes and thus afford a welcome alternative to the long-term oriented, yet quantitative and reductionist, rates-approach of organizational ecology as well as to the short-term-oriented and personality-focused traits-approach of entrepreneurship; this alternative setting permits researchers to abandon these misguided approaches without having to invent a new approach because the researchers can utilize already existing and well established settings.

This study leaves a number of challenges for future research. Among the most important are (a) the validation of the presented evolutionary core model of family business ecology and (b) the need for increasing the theoretical density of the proposed core model.

However, the closing comments of this research study will focus on the issue of imprinting; an issue about which the research community has very minimal knowledge, and which is paramount for a complete understanding of the evolution of organizations in general and family businesses in particular.

In Stinchcombe's view new organizational forms emerge not gradually, but in a radical manner, which is also known as quantum speciation or punctuated equilibrium[323]. One key assumption of Stinchcombe's argument is that some societies contain the conditions necessary for new forms[324] to emerge and others do not.[325] This, however, only shifts part of the *explanans* to the institutional structure and environment. His main argument for this explanation of new forms is based on the individual motivations of entrepreneurs[326].

---

[323] cf. Stinchcombe, 1965

[324] Stinchcombe in this context fails to differentiate between organizations and organizational forms

[325] Stinchcombe, 1965

[326] Stinchcombe, 1965

Aldrich refined this view by placing the analysis in the context of natural selection theory and by putting more emphasis on the institutional framework[327]. Both of these analyses, however, fall short of a sufficient explanation because Stinchcombe reduced the complex process of organizational founding to the motivations of the entrepreneur, while Aldrich reduced it to a number of specific characteristics that need to be in place in the environment for new organizational foundings to materialize.

McKelvey suggested viewing organizations as manifestations of competencies whose elements are temporarily embodied in the employees of organizations[328]. His view of newness is one of difference – different poolings of competencies[329]. This view of difference is analogous to the view of Luhmann, who suggests that the reduction to difference overrides and surpasses the view of reduction to selection[330].

Kauffman has argued from a biological perspective that all cells contain the same set of genes, yet all have different active genes[331].
If these arguments are applied to the context of this study, the following view might be adequate to explain origination and speciation. All family businesses are created with a similar set of competencies (to use McKelvey's construct). However, not all of these competencies are active at the same time since the institutional infrastructure determines which elements are within acceptable boundaries. An example from the proposed core model of family business is the element of incentives and motivators. If the proposed incentives are not permitted to be an equilibrated part of the family business system within the infrastructure, the values proposed could not be upheld and the formal creation of the organization might not be possible.

---

[327] Aldrich, 1979
[328] McKelvey, 1982:196
[329] McKelvey, 1982:275-276
[330] Luhmann, 1995:32
[331] Kauffman, 1995:24

These elements (or genes, or competencies), however, are not only found embodied in the employees. Certainly some of these elements are embodied in the employees, but others of these elements are found within the connections and connectors of this system, some of which might, for example, be called communication[332]. Further, speciation should be viewed, not as a definite event, but rather as a continuous process which is formally possible because the necessary elements (or genes, or competencies) are present, though all are not necessarily simultaneously active.

Luhmann suggested that, once identities are created, a continuous process of negotiation begins[333]. For an organization, this means continuous encounters with paradoxes, which are resolved through constant processes of de-paradoxification – de-paradoxification of the meaning of, and relationships between, the core elements. This continuous process of de-paradoxification leads, over time, to a better equilibrated system of core elements. If this process suggested by Luhmann is accepted, then it is a conceivable conclusion – and is here suggested – that 'sustainable success' could be a function of sufficient mastery of the internal de-paradoxification and equilibration process of the core elements. Finally, to paraphrase this explanation in one of Luhmann's metaphors: family businesses do not know if their core elements are what they state, but if they knew they would have to keep it to themselves[334].

---

[332] cf. Luhmann, 1994

[333] Luhmann, 1994

[334] cf. Luhmann, 1995:150-151; his exact wording is: "I don't know if I mean what I say. And if I knew, I would have to keep it to myself" Luhmann, 1994:387.

6. BIBLIOGRAPHY

Aldrich, H. E. 1979. *Organizations & Environments.* Englewood Cliffs: Prentice Hall.

Aldrich, H. E. 1990. Using an Ecological Perspective to Study Organizational Founding Rates. *Entrepreneurship: Theory & Practice* 14(3): 7-24.

Aldrich, H. E. 1999. *Organizations Evolving.* London: Sage.

Aldrich, H. E., & Auster, E. R. 1986. Even Dwarfs Started Small: Liabilities of Age and Size and their Strategic Implications. In L. L. Cummings & B. Staw (Eds.), *Research in Organization Behavior* (Vol. 8, pp. 165-198). Greenwich: JAI Press.

Aldrich, H. E., & Fiol, C. M. 1994. Fools Rush In? The Institutional Context of Industry Creation. *Academy of Management Review* 19(4): 645-670.

Aldrich, H. E., & Wiedenmayer, G. 1993. From Traits to Rates: An Ecological Perspective on Organizational Foundings. In J. A. Katz & R. H. Brockhaus, Sr. (Eds.), *Advances in Entrepreneurship, Firm Emergence, and Growth* (Vol. 1, pp. 145-195). Greenwich: JAI Press.

Aldrich, H. E., Zimmer, C. R., Staber, U. H., & Beggs, J. J. 1994. Minimalism, Mutualism, and Maturity: The Evolution of the American Trade Association Population in the 20th Century. In J. A. C. Baum & J. V. Singh (Eds.), *Evolutionary Dynamics of Organizations* (pp. 223-239). New York: Oxford University Press.

Amburgey, T. L., Dacin, T., & Kelly, D 1994. Disruptive Selection and Population Segmentation: Interpopulation Competition as a Segregation Process. In J. A. C. Baum & J. V. Singh (Eds.), *Evolutionary Dynamics of Organizations* (pp. 240-254). New York: Oxford University Press.

Amburgey, T. L., Kelly, D., & Barnett, W. P. 1993. Resetting the Clock: The Dynamics of Organizational Change and Failure. *Administrative Science Quarterly* 38: 51-73.

Amburgey, T. L., & Rao, H. 1996. Organizational Ecology: Past, Present, and Future Directions. *Academy of Management Journal* 39(5): 1265-1286.

Anderson, P. C., & Tushman, M. L. 1990. Technological Discontinuities and Dominant Designs: A Cyclical Model of Technological Change. *Administrative Science Quarterly* 35: 604-633.

Anonymous. 1994. Family values. *The Economist,* 331, 63.

Aronoff, C. E. 1998. Megatrends in Family Business. *Family Business Review* 11(3):181-5.

Ballarini, K., & Keese, D. 1995. *Die Struktur kleiner Familienunternehmen in Baden-Württemberg.* Heidelberg: Physica Verlag.

Barnett, W. P., & Amburgey, T. L. 1990. Do Larger Organizations Generate Stronger Competition? In J. V. Singh (Ed.), *Organizational Evolution* (pp. 78-102). Newbury Park: Sage.

Barnett, W. P., & Burgelman, R. A. 1996. Evolutionary Perspectives on Strategy. *Strategic Management Journal* 17(Summer Special Issue): 5-19.

Barnett, W. P., & Carroll, G. R. 1987. Competition and Mutualism Among Early Telephone Companies. *Administrative Science Quarterly* 32: 400-421.

Barnett, W. P., & Carroll, G. R. 1995. Modeling Internal Organizational Change. *Annual Review of Sociology* 21: 217-236.

Bateson, G. 1972. *Steps to an Ecology of Mind*. Frogmore, UK: Paladin.

Baum, J. A. C. 1996. Organizational Ecology. In S. R. Clegg, C. Hardy, & W. R. Nord (Eds.), *Handbook of Organization Studies* (pp. 77-114). London: SAGE.

Baum, J. A. C., & Mezias, S. J. 1992. Localized Competition and the Dynamics of the Manhattan Hotel Industry. *Administrative Science Quarterly* 37: 580-604.

Baum, J. A. C., & Oliver, C. 1996. Toward an Institutional Ecology of Organizational Founding. *Academy of Management Journal* 39(5): 1378-1427.

Baum, J. A. C., & Powell, W. W. 1995. Cultivating an Institutional Ecology of Organizations: Comment on Hannan, Carroll, Dundon, and Torres. *American Sociological Review* 60: 529-538.

Baum, J. A. C., & Singh, J. V. (Eds.). 1994a. *Evolutionary Dynamics of Organizations*. New York: Oxford University Press.

Baum, J. A. C., & Singh, J. V. 1994b. Organizational Niche Overlap and the Dynamics of Organizational Founding. *Organization Science* 5: 483-502.

Baum, J. A. C., & Singh, J. V. 1994c. Organizational Niche Overlap and the Dynamics of Organizational Mortality. *American Journal of Sociology* 100: 346-380.

Bechtle, C. 1983. *Die Sicherung der Führungsnachfolge in der Familienunternehmung*. Dissertation, HSG, St. Gallen.

Becker, P. H. 1993. Common Pitfalls in Published Grounded Theory Research. *Qualitative Health Research* 3: 254-260.

Bergamin, S. J. 1994. Bestandsgefährdende Faktoren im Familienunternehmen. *Internationales Gewerbearchiv*: 115-128.

Bergamin, S. J. 1995. *Der Fremdverkauf einer Familienunternehmung im Nachfolgeprozess*. Dissertation, HSG, St. Gallen.

Birley, S., & Sorensen, S. 1995, April. *The Family and the Business*. Paper presented at the 1995 Babson Entrepreneurship Research Conference, London Business School, London, UK.

Brittain, J., & Wholey, D. R. 1988. Competition and Coexistence in Organizational Communities. In G. R. Carroll (Ed.), *Ecological Models of Organization* (pp. 195-222). Cambridge, MA: Ballinger.

Brittain, J., & Wholey, D. R. 1989. Assessing Organizational Ecology as Sociological Theory: Comment on Young. *American Journal of Sociology* 95(2): 439-444.

Brockhaus, R. H., Sr. 1994a. Entrepreneurship and Family Business Research: Comparisons, Critique, and Lessons. *Entrepreneurship: Theory & Practice* 19(1): 25-38.

170

Brockhaus, R. H., Sr. 1994b. *Family Business Research: Entrepreneurship's Kissin' Cousin* (Paper presented to the 1994 AOM Entrepreneurship Division Doctoral Consortium). St. Louis: Jefferson Smurfit Center for Entrepreneurial Studies-Saint Louis University.

Brockhaus, R. H., Sr. 1994c. *Family Businesses: A Blessing or a Curse?* (Keynote Address given at the 1994 SEANZ Conference). St. Louis: Jefferson Smurfit Center for Entrepreneurial Studies-Saint Louis University.

Bruderer, E., & Singh, J. V. 1996. Organizational Evolution, Learning and Selection: A Genetic-Algorithm-Based Model. *Academy of Management Journal* 39(5): 1322-1349.

Brunner, J., Habersaat, M., & Pleitner, H. J. H. 1995. *Auslandsorientierung und Unternehmenspolitik schweizerischer Klein- und Mittelunternehmungen* (Ergebnisse der INTERSTRATOS-Erhebungen 1991-1994 in fünf Branchen). St. Gallen: Institut für gewerbliche Wirtschaft (IGW).

Bull, I., Thomas, H., & Willard, G. (Eds.). 1995. *Entrepreneurship: Perspectives on Theory Building.* Oxford, UK: Pergamon Press/Elsevier Science.

Bull, I., & Willard, G. E. 1993. Towards a Theory of Entrepreneurship. *Journal of Business Venturing* 8: 183-195.

Burgelman, R. A. 1996. Intraorganizational Ecology of Strategy Making and Organizational Adaptation: Theory and Field Research. In J. R. Meindl, C. Stubbart, & J. F. Porac (Eds.), *Cognition Within and Between Organizations* . Thousand Oaks: SAGE.

Burgelman, R. A., & Mittman, B. S. 1994. An Intraorganizational Ecological Perspective on Managerial Risk Behavior, Performance, and Survival: Individual, Organizational, and Environmental Effects. In J. A. C. Baum & J. V. Singh (Eds.), *Evolutionary Dynamics of Organizations* (pp. 53-75). New York: Oxford University Press.

Burt, R. S. 1992. *Structural Holes.* Cambridge, MA: Harvard University Press.

Bygrave, W. D. 1990a. The Entrepreneurship Paradigm (I): A Philosophical Look at Its Research Methodologies. *Entrepreneurship: Theory and Practice* 14(1): 7-26.

Bygrave, W. D. 1990b. The Entrepreneurship Paradigm (II): Chaos and Catastrophes among Quantum Jumps. *Entrepreneurship: Theory and Practice* 14(2): 7-30.

Bygrave, W. D. 1993. Theory Building in the Entrepreneurship Paradigm. *Journal of Business Venturing* 8(Special Issue): 255-280.

Caldwell, B. J. 1994. *Beyond Positivism.* (Revised ed.). London: Routledge.

Carroll, G. R. 1984. Organizational Ecology. *Annual Review of Sociology* 10: 71-93.

Carroll, G. R. 1985. Concentration and Specialization: Dynamics of Niche Width in Populations of Organizations. *American Journal of Sociology* 90: 1262-1283.

Carroll, G. R. (Ed.). 1988. *Ecological Models of Organization.* Cambridge, MA: Ballinger.

Carroll, G. R., & Hannan, M. T. 1990. Density Delay in the Evolution of Organizational Populations: A Model and Five Empirical Tests. In J. V. Singh (Ed.), *Organizational Evolution* (pp. 103-128). Newbury Park: Sage.

171

Carroll, G. R., & Wade, J. 1991. Density Dependence in the Organizational Evolution of the American Brewing Industry Across Different Levels of Analysis. *Social Science Research* 20: 217-302.

Chalmers, A. F. 1976. *What is this Thing called Science? : An Assessment of the Nature and Status of Science and its Methods*. St. Lucia, Queensland: University of Queensland Press.

Churchill, N. C., & Hatten, K. J. 1987. Non-Market-Based Transfers of Wealth and Power: A Research Framework for Family Business. *American Journal of Small Business* 11(3): 53-66.

Covin, J. G., & Slevin, D. P. 1997. High Growth Transitions: Theoretical Perspectives and Suggested Directions. In D. L. Sexton & R. W. Smilor (Eds.), *Entrepreneurship 2000* (pp. 99-126). Chicago: Upstart Publishing Co.

Crijns, H., Ooghe, H., & Cosaert, M. 1994, Nov. 24-25. *Transitions of Medium-Sized Family Companies*. Paper presented at the RENT VIII, Tampere.

Davis, P., & Stern, D. 1988. Adaptation, Survival, and Growth of the Family Business: An Integrated Systems Perspective. *Family Business Review* 1(1): 69-85.

de Chardin, T., SJ. 1995. Das Teilhard de Chardin Lesebuch. In G. Schiwy (Ed.) (2nd ed.). Olten: Walter-Verlag AG.

de Mello, A., SJ. 1984. *Wellsprings: A Book of Spiritual Exercises*. New York: Image Book.

Delacroix, J., & Carroll, G. R. 1983. Organizational Foundings: An Ecological Study of the Newspaper Industries of Argentine and Ireland. *Administrative Science Quarterly* 28: 274-291.

Denzin, N. 1978. *The Research Act: A Theoretical Introduction to Sociological Methods*. (2nd ed.). Chicago, IL: Aldine.

Denzin, N., & Lincoln, Y. (Eds.). 1994. *The Handbook of Qualitative Research*. Thousand Oaks, CA: SAGE.

Domayer, E., & Vater, G. 1994. Das Familienunternehmen - Erfolgstyp oder Auslaufmodell? *Hernsteiner - Fachzeitschrift für Management-Entwicklung*, 26-28.

Donckels, R. 1996a. *Family Businesses on Their Way to the Next Millennium* (Working Paper Presentation). Brussels: Catholic University Brussels.

Donckels, R. 1996b. The Fascinating World of Family Businesses: About Old Challenges in a Future-Oriented Perspective. *Southern African Journal for Entrepreneurship and Small Business* 8(2): 1-13.

Donckels, R., & Froehlich, E. 1991. Are Family Businesses Really Different? *Family Business Review* 4(2): 149-160.

Donckels, R., & Fröhlich, E. 1991. Sind Familienbetriebe Wirklich Anders? *Internationales Gewerbearchiv* 39(4): 219-235.

Donnelley, R. G. 1988. The Family Business. *Family Business Review* 1(4): 427-445.

Dreux IV, D. R. 1990. Financing Family Business: Alternatives to Selling Out or Going Public. *Family Business Review* 3(3): 225-245.

Dyer, W. G., Jr. 1994. Potential Contributions of Organizational Behavior to the Study of Family-Owned Businesses. *Family Business Review* 7(2): 109-131.

Dyer, W. G., Jr., & Handler, W. 1994. Entrepreneurship and Family Business: Exploring the connections. *Entrepreneurship: Theory & Practice* 19(1): 71-83.

Dyer, W. G., Jr., & Sanchez, M. 1998. Current State of Family Business Theory and Practice as Reflected in Family Business Review 1988-1997. Family Business Review 11(4): 287-95.

Dyer, W. G., Jr., & Wilkins, A. L. 1991. Better Stories, Not Better Constructs, To Generate Better Theory: A Rejoinder to Eisenhardt. *Academy of Management Review* 16(3): 613-619.

Eisenhardt, K. M. 1989. Building Theories from Case Study Research. *Academy of Management Review* 14(4): 532-550.

Eisenhardt, K. M. 1991. Better Stories and Better Constructs: The Case for Rigor and Comparative Logic. *Academy of Management Review* 16(3): 620-627.

Elfring, T., Jensen, H. S., & Money, A. (Eds.). 1995. *European Research Paradigms in Business Studies*. Copenhagen: Handelshojskolens Forlag.

Feyerabend, P. K. 1975. *Against Method: Outline of an Anarchistic Theory of Knowledge*. London: New Left Books.

Fiol, C. M., & Aldrich, H. E. 1995. Collusion or Collision? Exploring the Boundaries of Family Business. In A. L. Carsrud (Ed.), *UCLA Frontiers of Family Firm Research*. Los Angeles.

Fombrun, C. J. 1994. Taking on Strategy, 1-2-3. In J. A. C. Baum & J. V. Singh (Eds.), *Evolutionary Dynamics of Organizations* (pp. 199-204). New York: Oxford University Press.

Freeman, J., & Hannan, M. T. 1989. Setting the Record Straight on Organizational Ecology: Rebuttal to Young. *American Journal of Sociology* 95(2): 425-439.

Freeman, J., & Lomi, A. 1994. Resource Partitioning and Foundings of Banking Cooperatives in Italy. In J. A. C. Baum & J. V. Singh (Eds.), *Evolutionary Dynamics of Organizations* (pp. 269-293). New York: Oxford University Press.

Freund, W., Kayser, G., & Schröer, E. 1995. *Generationenwechsel im Mittelstand* (ifm-Materialien Nr. 109). Bonn: Institut für Mittelstandsforschung Bonn.

Fröhlich, E. 1992. *Jüngste empirische Ergebnisse zur Familienunternehmens- und Unternehmenstypenforschung*. Paper presented at the Rencontres de St-Gall, St. Gallen.

Fröhlich, E. 1995. Familie als Erfolgspotential im Gewerbe und Handwerk. In H. Stiegler (Ed.), *Erfolgspotentiale für KMU* (pp. 105-136). Linz: Universitätsverlag Rudolf Trauner.

Gallo, M. A. 1990. *The Role of the Wife in the Family Business* (192 BIS). Barcelona: IESE.

Gallo, M. A. 1991. *Family Business: Non-Family Managers* (220 BIS). Barcelona: IESE.

Gallo, M. A., & Estape, M. J. 1992a. *The Family Business among the Top 1000 Spanish Companies* (231 BIS). Barcelona: IESE.

Gallo, M. A., & Estape, M. J. 1992b. *The Internationalization of the Family Business* (230 BIS). Barcelona: IESE.

Gallo, M. A., & Estape, M. J. 1995. Family Businesses Among the Top 1000 Spanish Companies. In A. L. Carsrud (Ed.), *UCLA Frontiers of Family Firm Research*. Los Angeles.

Gallo, M. A., & Pont, C. G. 1988. *The Family Business in the Spanish Economy* (144). Barcelona: IESE.

Gallo, M. A., & Pont, C. G. 1993. *Important Factors in the Family Business Internationalization* (256 BIS). Barcelona: IESE.

Gallo, M. A., & Vilaseca, A. 1995, October 11-14, 1995. *Finance in Family Business*. Paper presented at the 1995 FFI Conference, St. Louis.

Gersick, K. E. 1994a. Handbook of Family Business Research, 1969-1994. *Family Business Review* 7(2): 103-107.

Gersick, K. E. 1994b. Reflections on the Family Business Literature: Pioneers Look to the Past and the Future. *Family Business Review* 7(2): 199-205.

Gersick, K. E., Davis, J. A., McCollom Hampton, M. & Lansberg, I. 1997. *Generation to Generation: Life Cycles of the Family Business*. Boston: Harvard Business School Press.

Ginsberg, A., & Baum, J. A. C. 1994. Evolutionary Processes and Patterns of Core Business Change. In J. A. C. Baum & J. V. Singh (Eds.), *Evolutionary Dynamics of Organizations* (pp. 127-151). New York: Oxford University Press.

Glaser, B. G., & Strauss, A. L. 1967. *The Discovery of Grounded Theory*. Chicago, IL: Aldine Publishing Co.

Goffe, R. 1996. Understanding Family Businesses: Issues for Further Research. *International Journal of Entrepreneurial Behaviour & Research*. 2(1):36-48.

Gracian, B., SJ. 1992. *Handorakel und Kunst der Weltklugheit* (Schopenhauer, Arthur, Trans.). (13. ed.). Stuttgart: Alfred Kröner Verlag.

Guba, E. 1990. *The Paradigm Dialog*. London: SAGE.

Guba, E. G., & Lincoln, Y. S. 1994. Competing Paradigms in Qualitative Research. In N. Denzin & Y. Lincoln (Eds.), *The Handbook of Qualitative Research* (pp. 105-117). Thousand Oaks, CA: SAGE.

Haahti, A. J. (Ed.). 1993. *INTERSTRATOS: Internationalization of Strategic Orientations of European Small and Medium Enterprises* (Institute Report 93-01). Brussels: European Institute for Advanced Studies in Management (EIASM).

Hamel, G., & Prahalad, C. K. 1994. *Competing for the Future*. Boston: Harvard Business School Press.

Handler, W. C. 1989. Methodological Issues and Considerations in Studying Family Businesses. *Family Business Review* 2(3): 257-276.

Handler, W. C. 1994. Succession in Family Business: A Review of the Research. *Family Business Review* 7(2): 133-157.

Handler, W. C., & Kram, K. E. 1988. Succession in Family Firms: The Problem of Resistance. *Family Business Review* 1(4): 361-381.

Hands, D. W. 1993. Popper and Lakatos in Economic Methodology. In U. Mäki, B. Gustafsson, & C. Knudsen (Eds.), *Rationality, Institutions & Economic Methodology* (pp. 61-75). London: Routledge.

Hannan, M. T. 1988. Age Dependence in the Mortality of National Labor Unions: Comparison of Parametric Models. *Journal of Mathematical Sociology* 14: 1-30.

Hannan, M. T., & Carroll, G. R. 1992. *Dynamics of Organizational Populations: Density, Legitimation, and Competition.* New York: Oxford University Press.

Hannan, M. T., & Carroll, G. R. 1995. Theory Building and Cheap Talk about Legitimation: Reply to Baum and Powell. *American Sociological Review* 60: 539-544.

Hannan, M. T., Carroll, G. R., Dundon, E. A., & Torres, J. C. 1995. Organizational Evolution in a Multinational Context: Entries of Automobile Manufacturers in Belgium, France, Germany, and Italy. *American Sociological Review* 60: 509-528.

Hannan, M. T., & Freeman, J. 1977. The Population Ecology of Organizations. *American Journal of Sociology* 82(March): 929-64.

Hannan, M. T., & Freeman, J. 1984. Structural Inertia and Organizational Change. *American Sociological Review* 49: 149-64.

Hannan, M. T., & Freeman, J. 1989. *Organizational Ecology.* Cambridge: Harvard University.

Hannan, M. T., Ranger-Moore, J., & Banaszak-Holl, J. 1990. Competition and the Evolution of Organizational Size Distributions. In J. V. Singh (Ed.), *Organizational Evolution* (pp. 246-268). Newbury Park: Sage.

Harris, D., Martinez, J. I., & Ward, J. L. 1994. Is Strategy Different for the Family-Owned Business? *Family Business Review* 7(2): 159-174.

Haveman, H. A., Baum, J. A. C., & Keister, L. A. 1996, August 11-14, 1996. *The Dynamics of Domain Overlap: Effects on Financial Performance, Growth, and Failure.* Paper presented at the 1996 Academy of Management Meeting, Cincinnati, OH.

Havemann, H. A. 1992. Between a Rock and a Hard Place: Organizational Change and Performance under Conditions of Fundamental Environmental Transformation. *Administrative Science Quarterly* 37: 48-75.

Havemann, H. A. 1993. Follow the Leader: Mimetic Isomorphism and Entry into New Markets. *Administrative Science Quarterly* 38: 593-627.

Hawley, A. H. 1950. *Human Ecology: A Theory of Community Structure.* New York: Ronald.

Hedberg, N. 1996. *The Evolution of the Petrol Dealing Industry in Finland.* Thesis, Lappeenranta University of Technology, Lappeenranta

Hinterhuber, H. H., Rechenauer, O., & Stumpf, M. (Eds.). 1994. *Die Mittelständische Familienunternehmung.* Frankfurt/Main: Peter Lang.

175

Hollander, B. S., & Elman, N. S. 1988. Family-Owned Businesses: An Emerging Field of Inquiry. *Family Business Review* 1(2): 145-164.

Holstein, J. A., & Gubrium, J. F. 1995. *The Active Interview*. (Vol. 37). Thousand Oaks: Sage.

Hoy, F. 1995. Strategic Management and the Family Firm. In A. L. Carsrud (Ed.), *UCLA Frontiers of Family Firm Research*. Los Angeles.

Hoy, F., & Verser, T. G. 1994. Emerging Business, Emerging Field: Entrepreneurship and the Family Firm. *Entrepreneurship: Theory & Practice* 19(1): 9-23.

Katz, J. A., Brockhaus, R. H., Sr., & Hills, G. E. 1993. Demographic Variables in Entrepreneurship Research. In J. A. Katz & R. H. Brockhaus, Sr. (Eds.), *Advances in Entrepreneurship, Firm Emergence, and Growth* (Vol. 1, pp. 197-236). Greenwich: JAI Press.

Kauffman, S. 1993. *The Origins of Order: Self-Organization and Selection in Evolution*. New York: Oxford University Press.

Kauffman, S. 1995. *At Home in the Universe: The Search for Laws of Self-Organization and Complexity*. New York: Oxford University Press.

Kennedy, P. 1993. *A Guide to Econometrics*. Cambridge, MA: MIT Press.

Kets de Vries, M. 1996. *Family Business: Human Dilemmas in the Family Firm*. London: International Thomson Business Press.

Kircherer, H.-P. 1997. Möglichkeiten zur Verbesserung der Entwicklungschancen mittelständischer Familienbetriebe durch die Einrichtung eines Beirats. In J. u. a. Belak (Ed.), *Unternehmensentwicklung und Management unter besonderer Berücksichtigung der Klein- und Mittelbetriebe in den Reformländern* (pp. 339-347). Zürich.

Klughardt, R., & Stöhlker, K. J. 1994. Besondere Risiken des Familienunternehmens. *CH-D-Wirtschaft*, 15-17.

Kuhn, T. 1970. *The Structure of Scientific Revolutions: International Encyclopedia of Unified Science*. (2nd ed.). (Vol. II). Chicago: University of Chicago Press.

Kuratko, D. F., Hornsby, J. S., & Montagno, R. V. 1993. Family Business Succession in Korean and U.S. Firms. *Journal of Small Business Management* 31(2): 132-136.

Ladner, A. 1996, 22.03.1996. Familien-Clans. *CASH*, 37-47.

Lakatos, I. 1970. Falsification and the Methodology of Scientific Research Programmes. In I. Lakatos & A. Musgrave (Eds.), *Criticism and the Growth of Knowledge* (pp. 91-116). Cambridge: Cambridge University Press.

Lakatos, I. 1978. *The Methodology of Scientific Research Programmes*. (Vol. 1). Cambridge: Cambridge University Press.

Lakatos, I., & Musgrave, A. (Eds.). 1970. *Criticism and the Growth of Knowledge*. Cambridge: Cambridge University Press.

Lank, A. G. 1996. *What do We mean by "A Family Business"?* (Working Paper). Lausanne: International Institute for Management Development (IMD).

176

Lansberg, I. 1995. Family Business: Field or Fad? In A. L. Carsrud (Ed.), *UCLA Frontiers of Family Firm Research*. Los Angeles.

Larsson, R. 1993. Case Survey Methodology: Quantitative Analysis of Patterns Across Case Studies. *Academy of Management Journal* 36(6): 1515-1546.

Lawrence, P. R., & Lorsch, J. W. 1967. *Organization and Environment*. Boston, MA: Harvard Business School Press.

Levinthal, D. A. 1991. Organizational Adaptation and Environmental Selection - Interrelated Processes of Change. *Organization Science* 2(1): 140-5.

Levinthal, D. A. 1995. *Adaptation in Rugged Landscapes* (Working Paper): The Wharton School.

Levinthal, D. A., & March, J. G. 1993. The Myopia of Learning. *Strategic Management Journal* 14: 95-112.

Litz, R. A. 1995. The Family Business: Toward Definitional Clarity. *Family Business Review* 8(Summer): 71-81.

Litz, R. A. 1997. The Family Firm's Exclusion From Business School Research: Explaining the Void; Addressing the Opportunity. *Entrepreneurship: Theory & Practice* 22(1):55-71.

Lomi, A. 1995a, September 28, 1995. *Ecological Theories of Organizations: A New Framework for Studying Entrepreneurship?* Paper presented at the Workshop on Innovation & Entrepreneurship, Copenhagen Business School, Copenhagen, Denmark.

Lomi, A. 1995b. The Population and Community Ecology of Organizational Founding: Italian Co-operative Banks, 1936-1989. *European Sociological Review* 11(1): 75-98.

Lomi, A., & Larsen, E. R. 1996. Interacting Locally and Evolving Globally: A Computational Approach to the Dynamics of Organizational Populations. *Academy of Management Journal* 39(5): 1287-1321.

Lorange, P. 1995. Creating a Learning Partnership: A Key to Competitive Advantage. *IMD Perspectives for Managers* (10, November 1995): 1-4.

Low, M. B., & MacMillan, I. C. 1988. Entrepreneurship: Past Research and Future Challenges. *Journal of Management* 14(2): 139-161.

Löwe, C. 1979. *Die Familienunternehmung - Zukunftssicherung durch Führung*. Dissertation, HSG, St. Gallen.

Luhmann, N. 1994. How Can the Mind Participate in Communication? In H. U. Gumbrecht & K. L. Pfeiffer (Eds.), *Materialities of Communication* (pp. 371-387). Stanford, CA: Stanford University Press.

Luhmann, N. 1995. *Social Systems* (Bednarz, John, Jr. with Baecker, Dirk, Trans.). Stanford, CA: Stanford University Press.

Lynn, L., & Rao, H. 1995. Failures of Intermediate Forms: A Study of the Suzuki Zaibatsu. *Organization Studies* 16: 55-80.

March, J. G., & Sproull, L. S. 1990. Technology, Management, and Competitive Advantage. In P. S. Goodman, L. S. Sproull, & a. Associates (Eds.), *Technology and Organizations* (pp. 144-173). San Francisco: Jossey-Bass.

Martin, J. 1990. Breaking up the Mono-Method Monopolies in Organizational Analysis. In J. Hassard & D. Pym (Eds.), *The Theory and Philosophy of Organizations* (pp. 30-43). London: Routledge.

Martinez, J. I., & Jimenez, P. 1995. Maintaining the Family Wealth while Maintaining the Family Firm: Strategic and Financial Considerations. In A. L. Carsrud (Ed.), *UCLA Frontiers of Family Firm Research*. Los Angeles.

McKelvey, B. 1982. *Organizational Systematics: Taxonomy, Evolution and Classification*. Berkeley, CA: University of California Press.

McKelvey, B. 1996, August 11-14, 1996. *Complexity vs. Selection among Coevolutionary Firms: A Complexity Theory of Strategic Organizing*. Paper presented at the 1996 Academy of Management Meeting, Cincinnati, OH.

Melin, L., & Hellgren, B. 1994. Patterns of Strategic Processes: Two Change Typologies. In H. Thomas, D. O'Neal, R. White, & D. Hurst (Eds.), *Building the Strategically-Responsive Organization*. Chichester: John Wiley & Sons.

Menard, S. W. 1995. *Applied Logistic Regression Analysis*. (Vol. Sage University Paper No. 106). Thousand Oaks, CA: SAGE Publications.

Meyer, J. W., & Rowan, B. 1977. Institutionalized organizations: Formal structure as myth and ceremony. *American Journal of Sociology* 83: 340-63.

Mezias, S. J., & Lant, T. K. 1994. Mimetic Learning and the Evolution of Organizational Populations. In J. C. Baum & J. V. Singh (Eds.), *Evolutionary Dynamics of Organizations*. New York: Oxford University Press.

Miles, M. B., & Huberman, M. A. 1994. *Qualitative Data Analysis*. (2nd ed.). Thousand Oaks: Sage.

Miner, A. S. 1994. Seeking Adaptive Advantage: Evolutionary Theory and Managerial Action. In J. A. C. Baum & J. V. Singh (Eds.), *Evolutionary Dynamics of Organizations* (pp. 76-89). New York: Oxford University Press.

Miner, A. S., Amburgey, T. L., & Stearns, T. M. 1990. Interorganizational Linkages and Population Dynamics: Buffering and Transformational Shields. *Administrative Science Quarterly* 35: 689-713.

Miner, A. S., & Haunschild, P. R. 1995. Population Level Learning. *Research in Organizational Behavior* 17: 115-166.

Miner, A. S., & Robinson, D. F. 1994. Organizational and Population Level Learning as Engines for Career Transitions. *Journal of Organizational Behavior* 15: 345-364.

Moore, J. F. 1993. Predators and Prey: A New Ecology of Competition. *Harvard Business Review*(May-June): 75-86.

Mugler, J. 1995. *Betriebswirtschaftslehre für Klein- und Mittelunternehmen*. (2. Ausgabe). Wien: Springer Verlag.

178

Neubauer, F. & Lank, A. G. 1998. *The Family Business: Its Governance For Sustainability*. London: Macmillan Press.

Nielsen, E., & Rao, H. 1992. An Ecology of Agency Arrangements: Mortality of Savings and Loan Associations: 1960-1987. *Administrative Science Quarterly* 37: 448-461.

North, D. C. 1990. *Institutions, Institutional Change and Economic Performance*. Cambridge: Cambridge University Press.

Perrow, C. 1986. *Complex Organizations: A Critical Essay*. (3rd ed.). New York, NY: Newbery Award Records.

Pfeffer, J. 1994. *Competitive Advantage through People*. Boston: Harvard Business School Press.

Pfeffer, J. M. 1993. Barriers to the Advance of Organizational Science: Paradigm Development as a Dependent Variable. *Academy of Management Review* 18: 599-620.

Pfeffer, J. M., & Salancik, G. R. 1978. *The External Control of Organizations: A Resource Dependence Perspective*. New York: Harper & Row.

Pindyck, R. S., & Rubinfeld, D. L. 1991. *Econometric Models & Economic Forecasts*. New York: McGraw-Hill.

Pine, A. 1992. *Das erfolgreiche Familienunternehmen*. Frankfurt/New York: Campus Verlag.

Pohlschröder, K. 1990, . Familienunternehmen stossen auf Vorurteile. *Unternehmermagazin*, 16-18.

Popper, K. R. 1934. *Logik der Forschung*: Springer Verlag.

Popper, K. R. 1985 (Original 1973). Evolutionary Epistemology. In D. W. Miller (Ed.), *Popper Selections* (pp. 78-86). Princeton, NJ: Princeton University Press.

Porter, M. E. 1985. *Competitive Advantage*. New York, NY: Free Press.

Porter, M. E. 1990. *Competitive Advantage of Nations*. New York, NY: Free Press.

Rommel, G., Brück, F., Diederichs, R., Kempis, R.-D., Kaas, H.-W., Fuhry, G., & McKinsey & Company, I. 1995. *Qualität Gewinnt*. Stuttgart: Schäffer-Poeschel Verlag.

Rosenbauer, C. 1994. *Strategische Erfolgsfaktoren des Familienunternehmens im Rahmen seines Lebenszyklus*. Dissertation, HSG, St. Gallen.

Rosenkopf, L., & Tushman, M. L. 1994. The Coevolution of Technology and Organization. In J. A. C. Baum & J. V. Singh (Eds.), *Evolutionary Dynamics of Organizations* (pp. 403-424). New York: Oxford University Press.

Schmoll, G. A. 1986. *Das Schweizer Familien-Unternehmen*. Genf: Market Development Publications.

Scott, W. R. 1995. *Institutions and Organizations*. Thousand Oaks: SAGE.

Seidel, M.-D. 1995. *Competitive Realignment in the Airline Industry* (Working Paper). Berkeley: Walter A. Haas School of Business, University of California at Berkeley.

179

Selz, M. 1996, December 13, 1996. Entrepreneurs may be more widespread than thought; survey finds 37% of U.S. households have taken a small-business flier. The Wall Street Journal, pp. B15A (E).

Sexton, D. L., & Kasarda, J. D. (Eds.). 1992. *The State of the Art of Entrepreneurship*. Boston, MA: PWS Kent Publishing Co.

Sexton, D. L., & Smilor, R. W. (Eds.). 1997. *Entrepreneurship 2000*. Chicago: Upstart Publishing Co.

Sharma, P., Chrisman, J. J. & Chua, J. H. 1997. Strategic Management of the Family Business: Past Research and Future Challenges. *Family Business Review* 10(1): 1-35.

Simon, H. 1996. *Die heimlichen Gewinner*. Frankfurt/Main: Campus Verlag.

Singh, J. V. (Ed.). 1990. *Organizational Evolution*. Newbury Park: Sage.

Spielmann, U. 1994. *Der Generationenwechsel in mittelständischen Unternehmungen bei Gründern und Nachfolgern*. Dissertation, HSG, St. Gallen.

Stacey, R. D. 1995. The Science of Complexity: An Alternative Perspective for Strategic Change Processes. *Strategic Management Journal* 16: 477-495.

Stinchcombe, A. 1965. Social Structure and Organizations. In J. G. March (Ed.), *Handbook of Organizations* (pp. 142-193). Chicago: Rand McNally.

Strauss, A., & Corbin, J. 1990. *Basics of Qualitative Research*. Newbury Park: Sage.

Swinth, R. L., & Vinton, K. L. 1993. Do Family-Owned Businesses Have a Strategic Advantage in International Joint Ventures? *Family Business Review* 6(1): 19-30.

Tagiuri, R. & Davis, J. A. 1992. On the Goals of Successful Family Companies. *Family Business Review* 5(1): 43-62.

Thompson, J. D. 1967. *Organizations in Action*. New York: McGraw-Hill.

Tushman, M. L., & Anderson, P. C. 1986. Technological Discontinuities and Organizational Environments. *Administrative Science Quarterly* 31: 439-465.

Tushman, M. L., & Romanelli, E. 1990. Organizational Evolution: A Metamorphosis Model of Convergence and Reorientation. In B. M. Staw & L. L. Cummings (Eds.), *The Evolution and Adaptation of Organizations* (pp. 139-190). Greenwich, CT: JAI Press.

Upton, N. B., & Heck, R. K. Z. 1997. The Family Business Dimension of Entrepreneurship. In D. L. Sexton & R. W. Smilor (Eds.), *Entrepreneurship 2000* (pp. 243-266). Chicago: Upstart Publishing Co.

Van de Ven, A. H. 1992. Longitudinal Methods for Studying the Process of Entrepreneurship. In D. L. Sexton & J. D. Kasarda (Eds.), *The State of the Art of Entrepreneurship* (pp. 214-242). Boston, MA: PWS Kent Publishing Co.

Van de Ven, A. H., & Garud, R. 1994. The Coevolution of Technical and Institutional Events in the Development of an Innovation. In J. A. C. Baum & J. V. Singh (Eds.), *Evolutionary Dynamics of Organizations* (pp. 425-443). New York: Oxford University Press.

Van de Ven, A. H., & Polley, D. 1992. Learning While Innovating. *Organization Science* 3(1): 92-116.

von Schultzendorff, D. 1984. *Fremdmanager in Familienunternehmen*. Dissertation, HSG, St. Gallen.

Wagner, V. 1994. *Die Gestaltung der Spitzenorganisation in der Familienunternehmung*. Bern: Berlin.

Walsh, F. 1994. Healthy Family Functioning: Conceptual and Research Developments. *Family Business Review* 7(2): 175-198.

Ward, J. L. 1986. *Family Ownership, Business Strategy and Performance: A Look at the PIMS Database*. Paper presented at the 1986 Academy of Management Conference.

Ward, J. L. 1995. The Family's Strategic Mission. In A. L. Carsrud (Ed.), *UCLA Frontiers of Family Firm Research*. Los Angeles.

Ward, J. L. 1997. Growing the Family Business: Special Challenges and Best Practices. *Family Business Review* 10(4): 323-37.

Ward, J. L., & Mendoza, D. S. 1994. *Global Perspectives on Family Business*, Loyola University Chicago.

Watkins, D. 1996. *How Relevant is the HRM Literature to Management Processes in the Family Firm?* Paper presented at the Rencontres de St-Gall 1996, St. Gallen.

Weick, K. E. 1995. *Sensemaking in Organizations*. Thousand Oaks, CA: SAGE Publications.

Welsch, H. P. 1997. *Family Business (from International Entrepreneurship and Small Business Bibliography)*. (2nd ed.). Chicago: DePaul University.

Widmer, U. 1995. Familienunternehmen benötigen eine Inhaberstrategie. *Der Organisator*, 6-9.

Williamson, O. E. 1975. *Markets and Hierarchies: Analysis and Antitrust Implications*. New York: Free Press.

Williamson, O. E. 1981. The Economics of Organization: The Transaction Cost Approach. *American Journal of Sociology* 87: 548-77.

Williamson, O. E. 1985. *The Economic Institutions of Capitalism*. New York: Free Press.

Williamson, O. E. 1993. Transaction Cost Economics and Organization Theory. *Industrial and Corporate Change* 2(2): 107-156.

Wimmer, R., Domayer, E., Oswald, M., & Vater, G. 1996. *Familienunternehmen - Auslaufmodell oder Erfolgstyp?* Wiesbaden: Gabler Verlag.

Winter, S. G. 1990. Survival, Selection, and Inheritance in Evolutionary Theories of Organization. In J. V. Singh (Ed.), *Organizational Evolution* (pp. 269-297). Newbury Park: Sage.

Wohlgemuth, A. C. 1993. Nachfolgeregelung im Familienunternehmen. *Neue Zürcher Zeitung* 14(19. Januar 1993): 31.

Wortman, M. S., Jr. 1986. A Unified Framework, Research Typologies, and Research Prospectuses for the Interface between Entrepreneurship and Small Business. In D. Sexton & R. Smilor (Eds.), *The Art and Science of Entrepreneurship* (pp. 273-331). Cambridge: Ballinger.

Wortman, M. S., Jr. 1987. Entrepreneurship: An Integrating Typology and Evaluation of the Empirical Research in the Field. *Journal of Management* 13(2): 259-279.

Wortman, M. S., Jr. 1995. A Typology of Family Firm Strategy. In A. L. Carsrud (Ed.), *UCLA Frontiers of Family Firm Research.* Los Angeles.

Wortman, M. S., Jr., & Birkenholz, W. 1990. *Entrepreneurship Research on a Global Basis: An Empirically based Model.* Paper presented at the 36th ICSB World Conference, Vienna.

Yin, R. K. 1989. *Case Study Research: Design and Methods.* London: Sage.

Young, R. C. 1988. Is Population Ecology a Useful Paradigm for the Study of Organizations? *Americal Journal of Sociology* 94(1): 1-24.

Young, R. C. 1989. Reply to Freeman and Hannan and Brittain and Wholey. *American Journal of Sociology* 95(2): 445-446.

Zaudtke, D., & Ammerman, D. 1997. Family Businesses: The Next Generation. *Management Review (of the AMA)* 86(No. 2 (February)): 55-57.

Zimmerer, C. 1991. Familienunternehmen - mehr Familie als Unternehmen? *Unternehmer Magazin*, 32-33.

Zucker, L. G. 1987. Institutional Theories of Organization. In W. R. Scott (Ed.), *Annual Review of Sociology* (Vol. 13, pp. 443-464).

Zucker, L. G. 1988. *Institutional Patterns and Organizations.* Cambridge: Ballinger.

Zucker, L. G. 1989. Combining Institutional Theory and Population Ecology: No Legitimacy, No History. *American Sociological Review* 54(4): 542-545.

182

Index

A

Aldrich, Howard 5, 23, 55, 56, 57, 168, 170, 174
Austria 62, 63, 69, 74, 75, 79, 90, 93, vii

B

Banks 178
Bateson, Gregory 67, 68, 171
Baum, Joel 6, 42, 49, 51, 53, 54, 57, 59, 170, 171, 172, 174, 175, 176, 178, 179, 180, 181
Brockhaus, Robert 2, 13, 22, 23, 28, 170, 171, 176
Bygrave, William 162, 172

C

Carroll, Glenn 48, 49, 50, 51, 54, 55, 56, 57, 170, 171, 172, 173, 175
Chardin, Teilhard de 1, 173
Complexity 176, 178, 179, 180
Constructivism, Social 58

D

Development 177, 179, 180, 181
Donckels, Rik 2, 17, 18, 19, 20, 173
Dyer, Gibb 2, 23, 26, 28, 41, 70, 173

E

Ecology 5, 48, 49, 170, 171, 172, 174, 176, 178, 179, 182, v
  organizational 5, 58
  population 48
Eisenhardt, Katharine 36, 41, 173, 174
Entrepreneur 180
Entrepreneurial 171
Environment 177
Epistemology 179
Europe 2, 7, 9, 11, 19, 61, 62, 66, 91, 92
European Union 7, 9, 59, 60, 61, 62, 63, 64, 65, 66, 68, 69, 73, 92, 164, vi, ix, x

183

F

Family business 2, 11, 12, 14, 15, 16, 19, 20, 81, 94, 95, 102, 105, 146, 163, 170, 171, 172, 173, 174, 175, 176, 177, 178, 179, 180, 181, 182, v, ix

ownership 91, 181

Family business form

dedication to 153, vii

incentive(s) 155, vii

simplicity 4, 149, 150, 152, vii

values 154, 155, vii

Feyerabend, Paul 45, 47, 59, 174, v

Freeman, John 5, 6, 8, 42, 43, 48, 49, 50, 51, 56, 87, 174, 176, 182

G

Gallo, Miguel 19, 174

Generation 93, 182

Germany 2, 4, 9, 16, 21, 62, 69, 74, 75, 80, 91, 92, 93, 150, 152, 175, vii, ix

Gersick, Kelin 12, 27, 174, 175

Glaser, Anselm 3, 4, 30, 31, 36, 39, 40, 41, 69, 85, 175

Grounded theory 3, 29, 32, 35, 36, v

coding 77, vi

Growth 170, 173, 176, 177

H

Hannan, Michael 5, 6, 8, 42, 43, 48, 49, 50, 51, 53, 54, 56, 57, 87, 171, 172, 174, 175, 176, 182

I

Innovation 97, 177, 181

Interview(s) 71, 176

K

Kuhn, Thomas 45, 46, 47, 177, v

L

Lakatos, Imre 8, 13, 42, 43, 44, 45, 46, 47, 85, 93, 175, 177

Lank, Alden 13, 14, 19, 20, 26, 28, 162, 177, 179

Lansberg, Ivan 11, 12, 177

Luhmann, Niklas 168, 169, 178

M

Management 1, 170, 171, 172, 173, 174, 175, 176, 177, 178, 179, 180, 181, 182

Market 180

McKelvey, Bill 4, 87, 150, 151, 168, 178

Mello, Anthony de 89, 173

Method(s) 47, 172, 173, 174, 181, 182

Methodology 67, 175, 177, vi

Mintzberg, Henry 1, 3, 4, 6, 9, 67

O

Ownership 91, 181

P

Popper, Karl 42, 45, 46, 47, 175, 179, v

Porter 5, 179, 180

Porter, Michael 5, 179, 180

Positivism 172

R

Regression 110, 113, 117, 119, 123, 126, 130, 133, 137, 141, 178, x

    Logit 108, 110, 115, 117, 121, 123, 128, 130, 135, 137, 145, x

    Probit 113, 119, 126, 133, 141, 145, x

Research methods

    qualitative 37, 171, 173, 175, 179, 180

    quantitative 177

S

Self-organization 176

Sociology 171, 172, 174, 175, 176, 178, 181, 182

Statistics 14, 105, 145, v, x

Sweden 62, 63, 69, 74, 75, 79, 92, 93, vii

Switzerland 9, 11, 15, 16, 68, 69, 74, 75, 79, 80, 92, 93, vii, ix
Systems 173, 178

T

Transition(s) 173, 179

V

Vision 163, 170, 175, 178, vii

W

Ward, John 14, 21, 25, 176, 181
Weick, Karl 4, 60, 150, 165, 181
Williamson, Oliver 6, 48, 181
Wortman, Max 24, 25, 28, 182

Z

Zucker, Lyn 54, 182

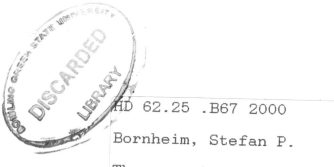